D0896398

WASHINGTON, ARKANSAS:

History on the Southwest Trail

by

MARY MEDEARIS

———————

Printed by
FIRMIN'S OFFICE CITY
formerly ETTER PRINTING CO.
Hope, Arkansas 71801

COPYRIGHT MARY MEDEARIS, 1976

(All rights reserved by the author)

Library of Congress No. A 794996

REVISED EDITION
September, 1984

THE SOUTHWEST TRAIL

N 1800 THE NARROW PATH of the Southwest Trail was the only public road through a wilderness that would become the State of Arkansas.

The line of this old Trail comes from the Mississippi River across a corner of Missouri, then due southwest for almost three hundred miles to the town of Fulton on the Red River. It cuts Arkansas in half as neatly as if someone had folded two triangles out of it — the mountainous regions in the upper triangle, the alluvial lands of the coastal plains in the lower triangle.

A branch of the Trail came across the Mississippi from where Memphis is now and joined the longer path in the middle of the territory.

The Trail has had many names. Perhaps it began as a buffalo trace, with the Indians following the buffalo. Perhaps it was used by the ancient Toltecs on their pilgrimages from Central Mexico. It is known that it was called the Chihuahua Trail when Spain held title to the land.

After the Louisiana Purchase in 1803 the United States Congress "improved" the Trail (by hacking away tree limbs and underbrush) and then it was called the Congress Road, or National Road.

When President Andrew Jackson had the Trail widened to 61 feet he used U.S. military troops for the labor and named it the Military Road.

After the Indians passed down the road on their way to the West it became part of the Trail of Tears.

In 1870 the railroad followed the line of the Trail.

Today, Highway 67 joins Interstate 30 near the Arkansas River and comes down the same old path — with a few deviations here and there.

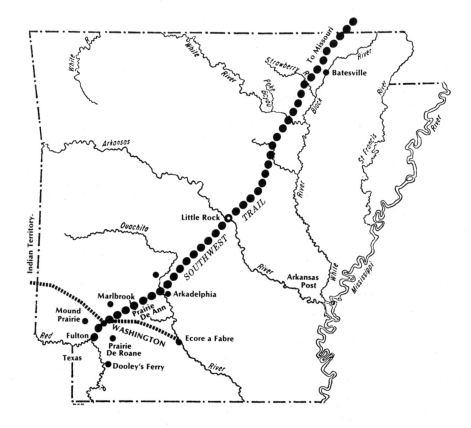

Map by Bert Smith

Route of the Southwest Trail from Missouri
through the Arkansas Territory in 1825.

THE HILL OF THE FIVE TRAILS

1819

HISTORY TRAVELED the Southwest Trail through this town of Washington, Arkansas; she came by foot, by horseback, by wagon train, by stagecoach — over the creek east of town, up the hill in front of the square white courthouse, past the crossroads where the tavern stands by the town well, on down through the hollow and into the setting sun.

The Big Red River was twelve miles down the Trail.

On the other side of Red River was Texas and the whole wide world.

Sam Houston rode over the Town Creek with a passport from Andrew Jackson in his saddlebags. Davy Crockett held a conversation with the tavern keeper at the town well. Jim Bowie wandered in and out — and in and out — and Stephen F. Austin came riding over the hill and down through the hollow before there was a tavern, or a town well, or even a courthouse there.

Stephen Austin came through in 1819. He was from Missouri. His brother-in-law James Bryan came with him.

The place where Washington is now was nothing more at that time than a landmark near the Red River where four Indian trails crossed the Southwest Trail on the top of a sandy pinehill.

There was only one "town" in the whole of the Arkansas Territory; it was the trading post on the Arkansas River, near the Mississippi River, where De Tonti had planted his post in 1686 while he was waiting for La Salle to meet him. There might have been four-hundred Anglo-Saxons in the Arkansas Post area — fur trappers and fur traders.

There were a few small settlements of white families along the other rivers, and on crossings of the Southwest Trail as it came down through the wilderness; settlements made with land grants given by the U.S. government to veterans of the Revolutionary War, and to young men who had fought in the War of 1812, and to a few settlers who had lost their lands in the great New Madrid earthquake in Missouri in 1811.

Otherwise, the forests were filled with Indians and wild beasts.

Two of these settlements of white families could be found near the hill of the five trails; Mound Prairie was one, five miles down the Indian

1

trail to the west and seven miles back on the Southwest Trail was a cluster of little log cabins around the main branch of the Ozan Creek.

Very few of the settlers had ventured down the two trails to the south; they led to a treeless prairie of dense canebrakes with very few springs. Here around the great sandhill were the gentle rolling lands, and it was here that the pioneers came with their cottonseed and their few slaves and set their first crude plantations in the rich black lands of the river bottoms and the creek bottoms.

The Territory of Arkansas had been created from the southern half of the Territory of Missouri on March 2, 1819. On April 18, the southwest portion of the Arkansas Territory was organized as the County of Hempstead. A "seat of justice" was located in the log home of John English in the settlement by the Ozan Creek — a settlement that would now be known as "Hempstead Court House."

By June, Stephen Austin and James Bryan were on their way down from Missouri.

They were not coming by way of the Southwest Trail. They took the water route. This way led by keelboat down the Mississippi River to the mouth of Red River, up Red River past the great 'raft' of floating logs and collected debris which made this route so perilous — and on to that far corner of the Arkansas Territory where the Southwest Trail came down to the Red River for the crossing into Spanish Territory.

Here there was a keelboat landing known as Fulton.

Moses Austin, Stephen's father, had made plans for that keelboat landing. Stephen and James Bryan would lay out a town site there and use it as a supply depot for the hundreds of cotton farmers who would come pouring into these delta lands now that the Arkansas Territory had been opened for settlers. Then, if Spain should decide to allow Moses Austin to found a colony of three hundred American families in that land across the Red River, the Austins reasoned that hundreds more settlers would come pouring through that crossing into the Province of Texas.

All they were waiting for was permission from the Spanish government.

At the moment Fulton was the jumping off place to nowhere. Nobody knew where the boundaries were over there and part of the land was in Arkansas Territory. There was also a buffer zone of twenty miles where no law existed from either the government of the United States, or of Spain — and outlaws harbored there, with warring Indian tribes roaming the plains, and Mexicans fighting to wrest their independence from Spanish rule.

The more cautious souls stayed on the Arkansas side of the Red River Valley.

When Stephen Austin and James Bryan landed their keelboat at the Fulton landing on that June day of 1819, they loaded their trunks and supplies onto pack mules and started up the Southwest Trail.

They knew where they were going. A few miles up the Trail they turned into a path blazed through the thick underbrush beneath the enormous trees and followed it to the settlement called Mound Prairie. Here they found a little Methodist log church named "Henry's Chapel", and the farm of the Reverend William Stevenson, Methodist preacher.

The Reverend Stevenson had come from the Austin corner of Missouri three years earlier. A whole colony of Methodists came with him; they had traveled by pack mules down the winding path of the Southwest Trail, cutting it a little wider as they came, and the families had scattered in the settlements around the hill of the five trails. Other friends from Missouri had arrived as early as 1812.

There were the five young Clark brothers, and the English brothers and the Wilson brothers and the Alexander brothers. There was John Johnson who would send for his brothers. There was William Shaw and his grown sons, and the Reed brothers and the Shook brothers and the Grounds brothers. Many of them were Methodist preachers and most of them had known Moses Austin of the Missouri lead mines, and Stephen, his son, who had served in the Missouri legislature.

Now Stephen and his brother-in-law James Bryan had come to open a plantation of their own. It was to be the first step in the plan for laying out a town site as a supply depot at the Fulton landing.

James Bryan bought the farm "Greenfields" from the Reverend William Stevenson for $900 (on credit.) Then he and Stephen unloaded their trunks and supplies and set to work.

The summer was hot and dry.

Neighbors helped James Bryan make "improvements" at Greenfields with his promises to pay them later. Another friend from Missouri,

3

Robert Andrews, helped with surveys for the town site at Fulton although very little could be done there until the Conway brothers, Henry and James, came down from Missouri to make the federal land surveys.

Stephen seemed to live on his horse! His trunk stayed at Greenfields but he was back and forth on the Southwest Trail — sixty miles back to the crossing on the Ouachita River, and a hundred-and-twenty miles back to the crossing on the Arkansas River — working to establish land claims for two more town sites to use as supply depots.

In November he suddenly decided to run for delegate to Congress in the first election to be held in the Arkansas Territory. There was very little time in which to campaign; the election was only thirteen days away.

But the Austins were beginning to feel a few money concerns. James Bryan's plantation was incurring debts. Stephen had come with $1,500 in borrowed gold in his saddlebags. They were gambling on the legality of a few New Madrid land certificates which Moses Austin had managed to salvage from the crash of the St. Louis bank that had bankrupted their Missouri lead mines in 1817.

They were also gambling on a few Missouri friends who were beginning to become influential in Arkansas politics. Three of those friends were from the settlements around the great sandhill. David Clark and John English and the Reverend William Stevenson had been appointed as representatives from Hempstead County to attend the Special Territorial Assembly to meet at the Arkansas Post in February of 1820. At that meeting the Reverend William Stevenson would make a motion that the capital of the new territory be located at the site of "the little rock" — and "the little rock" was the crossing of the Southwest Trail at the Arkansas River where Stephen had chosen his town site.

Things looked rather bright for the Austins.

Nothing at all turned out right.

On November 20 when the election was held for the first delegate to Congress from the Arkansas Territory, Stephen Austin ran second; he had filed too late for his name to appear on the ballot in two of the five counties.

By springtime, even before the General Assembly met at the Arkansas Post to choose the site for the capital, the Austins knew they would lose in their land claims at the Ouachita and Arkansas Rivers; those New Madrid land certificates were not valid on land south of the Arkansas River.

4

In April an auction was held for the sale of town lots in Fulton on Red River "...the point at which the most direct road leading from the Territory of Missouri to the extensive and fertile Province of TEXAS will cross said river..." and nobody rushed to buy. The Conway brothers had not been down to finish the federal land surveys — but who would want to buy town lots where the banks of the Red River could not be trusted when high waters came? The Red was well noted for overflows.

In June the ledger was tallied up for the year at the plantation; the results of the hot dry summer of 1819 were disastrous. Neighbors were already riding over the hill of the five trails to attend the June term of the Court of Common Pleas at Hempstead Court House to sue James Bryan for improvements at Greenfields that had never been paid for. Even the Reverend Stevenson pointed out that Greenfields had not been paid for in the first place.

In July an encouraging event happened: the new governor, James Miller, appointed Stephen as judge of the First Circuit Court; then the Second Territorial Assembly met at the Arkansas Post in the autumn and reorganized the government and abolished that position.

There was nothing left in Arkansas for the Austins. James Bryan went back to Missouri. Stephen caught a boat for New Orleans — he left so fast that he did not even take time to go back to Mound Prairie and get his trunk from Greenfields.

And as Stephen Austin was traveling down the Mississippi River toward New Orleans to await further plans from his father, their friend, the Reverend William Stevenson, was building a huge log shed on the side of the sandy pinehill by the Black Bois d'Arc creek. The shed was to be used as a place to hold Methodist revival camp meetings.

The Reverend Stevenson called his hill "The Ebenezer Camp Ground.

The hill of the five trails was the logical choice for a camp meeting ground. It was no more than a half-day journey by oxcart from any of the little settlements near the Red River.

Many oxcarts had begun to appear on the Southwest Trail and along the Indian paths in the forests. For the past year and a half the Court of Common Pleas had been appointing men to get out with their slaves and their axes and lay off roads from Hempstead Court House to Ozan (a new settlement on one of the three forks of the Ozan Creek), from Ozan to Mound Prairie, from Mound Prairie to a settlement growing at Columbus, from Columbus on down to Fulton on Red River. Underbrush had been cleared away, tree stumps leveled to six inches above the ground.

Travelers constantly came riding over the big sandy pinehill and on down to the Red River to contemplate taking their chances on the other side. Many crossed over. Many turned back. The land was called "Mexico" over there now; the Mexicans had won their fight with Spain but the outlaws and the Indians were as dangerous as ever.

A town grew up around the shed of the Ebenezer Camp Ground without anyone noticing at first.

Elijah Stuart came and built a tavern on the rise of the hill where the weary traveler could see an overnight accomodation as soon as he had crossed over the creek. William Shaw and his two sons placed a blacksmith shop nearby; they were to re-tire wagons and shoe horses, while a young silversmith named James Black, from Philadelphia, was brought in as a partner to repair guns and forge knives.

John Johnson brought his partner Abraham Block and built a mercantile store (with coffees and cambrics from New Orleans) near the point where the five trails crossed. Ephraim Mirick and Matthew Moss set a trading post on the other side of the Trail.

More log houses were appearing here and there. William Trimble, the first prosecuting attorney for the Territory of Arkansas, had arrived and married one of the six daughters of Abraham Stuart, brother to Elijah. Henry and James Conway were busy in the area with their surveying tools at last. A young schoolmaster from Kentucky, Daniel Witter, announced the opening of a one-room log schoolhouse at Hempstead Court House. Dr. Nathan Smith, from Connecticut, built a circle of little cabins to serve as a hospital on his farm at Mound Prairie where his mulberry trees were growing for his silkworms.

John Johnson went out one day with a crew and cut a road of his own straight southeast across the Prairie d'Ann from the Black Bois d'Arc creek to the settlement of Ecore a Fabre on the Ouachita River. Now the farmers could haul their cotton overland to the Ouachita River, and down that route to the market at New Orleans, circumventing the monstrous raft of fallen trees and silt-laden debris that created a riverman's nightmare on the Red River.

In these years of 1822, 1823 and 1824 the Ebenezer Camp Ground had become the seat of Methodism in Arkansas Territory: the Reverend William Stevenson had gathered together the Arkansas Methodist District Conference to meet on the hill of the five trails, and William Stevenson himself would become known as the "Father of Methodism" on Arkansas soil.

The Rev. Stevenson wrote to Stephen Austin on Oct. 5, 1823 to remind him of a trunk left at Greenfields. He sent the letter with a traveler on his way up the Southwest Trail to Missouri:

> Dr. Sr.
>
> Having heard a verbal visit of your return from Mexico and an opportunity offering of writing I have embraced it. I had agreed with Mr. John Clark last winter to freight your trunk to N. Orleans according to your wishes but the boat started somewhat sooner than expected owing to a sudden rise in the water having prevented me from complying with this promise. I could have sent it with some others but I did not think it prudent as there had been many threats against it as your property. The people in this County have been somewhat sickly this season and I think many will remove to Texas if they are not discouraged by something yet unknown.....

Stephen was busy founding a colony on the Brazos River in the Mexican province of Texas. His father had been granted the right by Spain to plant a colony of three-hundred American families in Texas — a grant which Mexico had honored — but it was Stephen who was leading them there. Moses Austin had died. Stephen was taking them by way of the water route and through Natchitoches, Louisiana.

Several of the families from the settlements on the Arkansas side of the Red River were preparing to follow the old Spanish Trail and join the colony on the Brazos River. Robert Andrews, who had helped with the surveys at Fulton, delayed his departure long enough to serve as the representative from Hempstead County in the 1821 General Assembly, and urge that the "permanent seat of justice" for Hempstead County be located at the "the place at the head of Bodark."

In the spring of 1824 the Congress of the United States granted three-quarters of a section of land to all counties in the Territory of Arkansas for the location of a permanent seat of justice. In the autumn of that year the Court of Common Pleas for Hempstead County was held in the tavern of Elijah Stuart, on the hill of the five trails. A decision had been made to locate the permanent seat of justice at "the place at the head of Bodark."*

Tilman L. Patterson was ordered by the court to build a courthouse.

In March 1825, at the term of the Court of Common Pleas, the clerk wrote in the long thin book that held the court records:

> It appearing to the satisfaction of the Court that three of the commissioners of the County of Hempstead, Elijah Stuart, John Nunn and James Moss, have caused a courthouse to be built at the seat of

*The Black Bois d'Arc Creek.

justice by Tilman L. Patterson for which they were to pay the said
Patterson $250 the said commissioners are ordered to pay the said Pat-
terson the said $250.

The first Hempstead County courthouse had been placed on the very crown of the hill. It was built of logs hewn from the giant pines of the forest.

On May 23, 1825, Col. John Clark wrote a letter from the new court-house to his friend Stephen F. Austin. He sent it with a traveler on his way down the Southwest Trail to the Brazos River:

> Dear Austin:
> A gentleman has just called at our court house who says he is going to your settlement in Texas, consequently I have but a moment to write. I have at last got possession of your trunk and I suppose the most of your books but the trunk has been broke open and I expect some articles taken out of it. The trunk was at Vaughn's and after his death a scoundrel by the name of Fields married the widow who denied having it but it was after discovered by administrators of Vaughn's estate...''

After five years, John Clark and the Reverend Stevenson finally got Stephen Austin's trunk across the Red River — but the Reverend Steven-son was getting ready to cross the Red River himself. After spending ten years of his life spreading Methodism throughout the entire southern half of the Arkansas Territory he was now going to spend the next ten years of his life becoming the "Father of Methodism" in Claiborne Parish, Louisiana.

Col. John Clark found time to add another paragraph in his letter to Stephen Austin on that day of May 23, 1825.

> "..If you know anything of Robert Andrews, for God's sake let me hear of him. I feel interested in Andrews and would like to know that he is doing well. If he is with you, tell him we have a flourishing little village at the place he was endeavoring to get the seat of justice located at for this county, on the head of Bodark, called WASHINGTON...."

Over on the Brazos River, in the Mexican province of Texas, there was a new settlement of American families called WASHINGTON-ON-THE-BRAZOS.

The destinies of the two towns would be entwined inexorably for the next ten years.

JAMES BLACK, THE SILVERSMITH OF THE BOWIE KNIFE

1831

THERE HAD BEEN a beautiful love story on the hill of Washington during the years 1820 to 1830. James Black, the young silversmith from Philadelphia whom William Shaw had brought in as a partner to repair guns and forge knives in his blacksmith shop, had fallen in love with William Shaw's only daughter, Anne.

It had not been a smooth romance. James Black had left town for a few years after William Shaw refused to allow his daughter to marry a lowly hired hand with no background when she could have a choice from among the young men in the plantations around the hill.

James Black had gone over to the Rolling Fork of the Little River, near the western boundary of the Arkansas Territory, where two of the Clark brothers, James and Gilbert, were operating a salt works.

Anne had said she would wait.

James Black thought he had sold back his share of the partnership in the blacksmith shop to William Shaw, to be repaid later. James had borrowed funds from friends to start his new project. He built a dam, set up a grist mill, and began work on a blacksmith shop.

Then the U.S. government ordered a new survey of the western boundary in 1824; Indians were to be removed west of the Arkansas Territory in a few years. When the new line was surveyed by James Sevier Conway it was found that the dam, the grist mill and the blacksmith shop were in Indian Territory; so were the salt works owned by the Clark brothers. The white men were ordered to leave.

James and Gilbert Clark crossed the Red River where they would found the town of Clarksville in a few years.

James Black came back to Washington. He needed to collect his money from William Shaw. He had friends to repay.

Something had gone wrong — William Shaw said there was no money due from the old partnership. There was nothing left to do but for James Black to go back to work for William Shaw — and that was a mistake. Anne was just around the corner.

9

Two years later, so the story goes, James Black had repaid all his debts and again he asked for permission to marry Anne. Again her father said "No."

At last, in 1828, James Black and Anne Shaw walked over to the log courthouse on the crown of the hill and were married by the clerk of the court, without her father's consent. Then they built a home next door to William Shaw; surely he would relent and give them his blessing when he could see that James was now able to build his own blacksmith shop and provide a slave for Anne's comfort.

But William Shaw never forgave his daughter.

A year went by and a son was born to James and Anne Black. He was named William for his grandfather.

The new blacksmith shop prospered. James Black's knives had become the wonder of the men on the Southwest Trail. Travelers would wander up to the doorway of the shop to watch the young smithy at work. At last James Black hung a shield of a leather apron between himself at the forge and the curious eyes in the shop, so no one could discover the secret processes by which he tempered the blades of his knives.

Then one December day in 1831, the tall wandering man, James Bowie, came up the Southwest Trail from the direction of the Red River and asked James Black to make a knife for him. It must be a large knife, he said, and a powerful knife — powerful enough to sever the head of a deer with one stroke.

James Bowie had drawn a design for the knife he wanted. He would return for the finished knife in January.

In January, when James Bowie came back down the Southwest Trail, James Black had two knives ready to show him. One was a knife made from the design James Bowie had left — the other was a knife made by a design created by James Black.

James Bowie tested the two knives. He decided to buy the one of James Black's design. He paid for the new knife, mounted his horse and rode on down the Trail toward the Red River.

James Black's new knife would become famous the world over but from this moment it would be known simply as a "bowie."

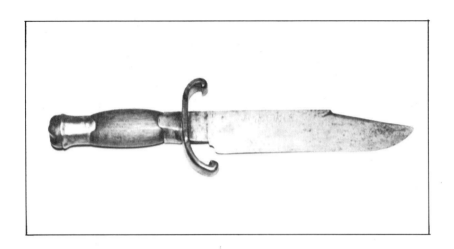

This Bowie knife, owned by Bart Moore, is believed to be an original Bowie made by James Black for Jim Bowie. At left is a close-up of the "maker's mark" showing a J B in an acorn.

THE INDIAN REMOVAL
1832 — 1838

IN JANUARY OF 1832 the first of the long lines of Indians came walking up the road past the log courthouse. Indians had been coming through the town for the past few years, sometimes only a single family, sometimes a group with a chieftain, but now the Choctaw Indians came by the thousands and they came with U.S. government agents.

Andrew Jackson was President of the United States. He had campaigned for that office on the promise to remove all Indians east of the Mississippi River to lands west of the Arkansas Territory.

Plans had been made for years for this Indian removal. Thousands of dollars had been appropriated by Congress to widen the Southwest Trail to accommodate the caravans. In the summer of 1831 a notice appeared in the Arkansas Gazette, in Little Rock, the only newspaper in the Territory:

> Sealed proposals received through the P.O. at Washington, Ark., for opening Road to be opened 61 feet wide — bridges erected where streams require it — all swampy ground to be causewayed. Bids to be in by August 15th.

A new road was to come from Fort Jessup in Louisiana to intersect the Southwest Trail by the Black Bois d'Arc creek. Work would commence by September 1st.

In December, while the U.S. military troops were still working on the road, the first 1,200 Choctaws were gathered at the Arkansas River, near Little Rock, ready to make their march toward the Indian Territory.

It was one of the coldest of all winters. The swamps were icy mud; the roads were frozen ruts. "The roads are horrid, horrid in the extreme," wrote Captain Jacob Brown to his superiors: "I have large companies repairing the roads and making bridges on the route, but notwithstanding this, the roads will continue to be horrid."

To make the journey even more wretched for the Indians — they were half naked. They had never been accustomed to wearing many clothes in the warm climates where they had lived and no one had provided them with covering for this cold weather. Very few of the Indians wore moccasins. Most of them were barefooted, and they were walking.

12

Cholera had broken out at Vicksburg, on the Mississippi River, where they had first been gathered together by government agents. When the wagons came rumbling over the hill of Washington, with the sick and dying in the wagons, the townspeople shut their doors. They were fearful; white drivers had contracted cholera, too.

Some of the plantation owners around the hill became rich at this time. They had secured government contracts to supply food for the Indians along the route. They brought ears of corn from their fields, and cattle from the barns, and met the caravans at stands set up in advance along the Southwest Trail. They pocketed the payment from the agents in charge and went home to wait for the next migration to come through.

In February there were nine hundred more Choctaws, with the family of the chief Nitakechi dying in his wagon.

Measles, as well as cholera, raged up and down the Mississippi River through that spring and summer. In the autumn there were more Choctaw Indians, and this time the plantation owners did not bother to deliver the supplies in person — corn was dumped by the side of the Trail and emaciated cattle left tethered to stakes nearby.

For two years the Choctaws came through Washington by way of the two Military Roads, and then there was only a trickling of Indians for a few years — until 1837, when it was time for the removal of Chickasaw Indians. Then it was the Chickasaws who came through by the hundreds, day after day, month after month.

The Chickasaws had money. Several of the merchants on the hill became rich at this time.

A young German adventurer named Frederick Gerstaecker, who had been traveling in the Arkansas Territory during these years, wrote in his Journal:

> Their trail was easy to follow. Numerous square holes cut in the fallen trees showed where the Squaws had pounded their maize to make bread. More melancholy traces were visible in the bones of human beings and animals that were strewed about. Many a warrior and Squaw died on the road from exhaustion: and the maladies engendered by their treatment; and their relations and friends could do nothing more for them than fold them in their blankets and cover them with boughs and bushes to keep off the vultures, which followed their route by thousands and soared over their heads; for their drivers would not give them time to dig a grave and bury their dead. The wolves, which also followed at no great distance, soon tore away so frail a covering, and scattered the bones in all directions..

As the Indians walked over the hill of Washington and down through the hollow, there were two directions they could take to their new lands in the Indian Territory. The road to the right led to Fort Towson beyond the western boundary; the other road led through Fulton and across Red River into the plains of Texas. It made no difference which road the Indians took — both roads had become part of the Trail of Tears.

SAM HOUSTON GOES TO TEXAS

1832

ANDREW JACKSON'S shadow was over everything in 1832: it rode down the Southwest Trail in November with a tough, rough, whisky-drinking giant who carried a passport bearing the seal of the President of the United States. The passport read:

> He is six feet three inches tall, has chestnut hair, blue eyes and fair skin. The U.S. will expect all Indian tribes..to permit Gen. Sam Houston to pass freely through their territories...

Gen. Sam Houston wore a Mexican poncho slung over his shoulders and there were solid silver plates on his saddle. He was on his way for a peace-making journey among the Indian tribes in Texas.

There is a legend in the town, handed down from father to son and from son to grandson, that Sam Houston met with Stephen Austin and James Bowie in Washington at this time to plot the liberation of Texas from Mexican tyranny.

Legend also has it that as Sam Houston was leaving the town he rode toward the Red River with the U.S. Marshal, Elias Rector, who had been holding court in Washington. The two men intended to part company at the river, and as they traveled the miles down the Trail they whiled away the hours with a jug of whisky from a Washington tavern.

Nearing the river, Sam Houston remarked that the scrawny, tailless mustang that he rode was a most humiliating mount for a man to be seen upon when he was riding into Texas to see friends for the first time, and Elias Rector offered to exchange horses with him. Elias was riding a beautiful bay horse. Elias then searched through his saddlebags and wished aloud that he could find a gift to give his friend in this momentous moment of parting — but all he could see to give was an old razor. That would be fine, Houston said — he would take the razor as a gift — and furthermore, if everything went as he thought everything was going to go over yonder, Elias would hear some day that his old razor was shaving the face of the President of the Republic of Texas!

Whereupon Elias Rector turned the tailless mustang in the direction of Fort Towson, in the Indian Territory, and Sam Houston rode the beautiful bay horse across the Red River into Texas, where he spent his first night at the home of James and Isabella Clark.

15

It is a matter of record that it was the date of December 10, 1832, when the ferry carrying Sam Houston into Texas tied up to a cottonwood stump on the south side of Red River. It is also a matter of record that four days later, on December 14, James Bowie was galloping over the plains of east Texas with "100 volunteers from the Red River plantations", on their way toward Fort Towson, when word had been sent that Comanches were on the warpath in the direction of the fort. If James Bowie and Sam Houston had not met in Washington a few days previous to these December days, they were mighty close together now in this corner of the world where James Clark's wife, Isabella, was a kinswoman to Stephen F. Austin.

And it is another well-known fact that four months later, in April of 1833, Gen Sam. Houston and Capt. James Bowie were riding together, in company with several other men, on their way to Washington-On-The-Brazos, after attending a convention at San Felipe where a resolution had been passed to separate Texas from the Republic of Mexico.

A RENDEZVOUS IN WASHINGTON

November — 1834

BY 1834 THERE WERE several frame houses in the town of Washington. John Johnson had built a sawmill on the Mine Creek in 1829. Owners of the plantations around the hill began to build town-houses for themselves in Washington.

Those pioneer homes on the plantations had been constructed of logs and built on the two-pen plan — two separate rooms with an open hallway between. Now the builders began to improve on the design.

Abraham Block, the wealthy Jewish merchant, built his Washington home two storys high with floors made of hand hewn timbers and Federal interior trim and mantelpieces. Mrs. Frances Isaacs Block had refused to leave her home in New Orleans until the new house was ready — then she came with her three children and her rosewood furniture, her silver and fine china, her silks and her linens, and joined her husband in the frontier wilderness of the Arkansas Territory.

It was still a rough country. Bears and panthers still roamed the canebrakes. Every day someone died of the chills and the fevers and was buried in the cemetery in the hollow behind Abraham Block's new home.

The Southwest Trail was still a difficult and dangerous road to travel, with robbers to wait for the unwary, and no accommodations along the way for the traveler to take a room for the night; he had to depend upon a knock at the door of any cabin he came to when the sun was setting. If no cabin was in sight he spread his blankets under the stars and hoped he would still be alive the next morning.

Sometimes even the roof of a cabin did not mean safety. Old Nicholas Trammell, who had blazed his own Trammell's Trace in 1813 to run stolen horses and slaves from Louisiana and Texas, had retired to a tavern on the road to Camden (once known as Ecore a Fabre) where he welcomed visitors in for the night — but soon it began to be whispered about that the footsteps of several lone travelers had been traced as far as Nick Trammell's cabin where they had vanished forever.

Yet still the travelers came on — and now and then a young man from Europe would come wandering up the hill past the log courthouse and say he had come to see what could be in this far corner of the fascinating land west of the Mississippi River. Then the young man would turn around and go back to Europe and publish an account of his journeys in America.

One of these European travelers was an Englishman named George William Featherstonhaugh (pronounced "Fenshawe"). His wanderings brought him through Washington in the autumn of 1834, at the same time that Sam Houston was back from his peace-making journey among the Texas Indians.

Sam Houston had been in Washington D.C., in January of 1834, talking with President Andrew Jackson. Now, in November, here he was again — exactly where he had been two years before to the month — drinking and gambling in an upper room of the tavern by the town well.

Several of Sam Houston's friends seemed to be in town at the same time; they said they were here to take advantage of the land sales going on in Washington, but their heavy boots could be heard clumping up and down the outside steps of the tavern at all hours of the day and night.

On a sunny afternoon in late November, Mr. Featherstonhaugh was several miles back on the Southwest Trail, picking up fossils and plant specimens to take back for a geological report to the U.S. government. Mr. Featherstonhaugh planned to arrive at the home of Judge Edward Cross by nightfall; he carried a letter of introduction.

Edward Cross was married to the gentle Laura Frances Elliott, of the Elliotts of Old Virginia, and they lived on a plantation they called "Marlbrook", in the area where the first courts for Hempstead County had been held.

Mr. Featherstonhaugh was in for a pleasant surprise. For the past several days he had been making his way down the Southwest Trail from Missouri, spending the nights in cabins as they appeared, and becoming more and more appalled (and slightly bemused) by the crude manners and primitive living conditions of the people he met. Now he was to become completely charmed with his accommodations for the next few days. He was also to become rather apprehensive about a few other things he would notice while he was in the vicinity.

George William Featherstonhaugh's journal of his "Excursions Through the Slave States of North America" was published in England in 1844:

> After riding for seven miles through a pretty good country, I turn-
> ed off to the left, to a gentleman's by the name of Judge Cross, to

whom I had a letter of introduction. He was a Judge under the U.S. Government, and had jurisdiction as far as the Mexican frontier. The house was on a knoll about half a mile from the road, and I reached it a little after dark.

Fastening my horse to a paling which surrounded a neat looking wooden house, built upon the double-cabin plan, I entered the court-yard, and then the open space that separates the two cabins. There was a cheerful light in the room to the right, and, knocking at the door with a pilgrim's feeling, I modestly entered a neat parlour, and saw a lady and two gentlemen sitting near a blazing fire.

Pleasing as the aspect of all this was, that which really astonished me was a piece of furniture my wondering eyes could scarce give credit to — a real carpet! I now felt doubly full of respect for everybody and everything, and, without venturing upon the carpet, I enquired if the Judge was at home. Upon this, a gentlemanly-looking person, about thirty-five years old, rose, and said he was Judge Cross. I now presented my letter, which being read, the most unaffected kind reception was given me, and in five minutes I had the satisfaction of know-ing my good horse Missouri was taken care of, and of forming one of the family circle.

Mrs. Cross was a lady-like and agreeable woman; full of the most amiable attentions to me. The supper was excellent, and the evening was concluded by a very instructive conversation I had with the Judge on the movements which for some time I had not been able to shut my eyes upon, in relation to the Mexican province of Texas.

This exceedingly increased my desire to see more of this southern country in company with the Judge, so, next morning after breakfast he very obligingly mounted his horse, and we made an agreeable ex-cursion in the neighbourhood, calling for a short time at the little in-significant village of Washington, where the government land sales were holding.

I was not desirous of remaining long at this place. General Houston was here, leading a mysterious sort of life, shut up in a tavern, seeing nobody by day, and sitting up all night. The world gave him credit for passing these his waking hours in the study of "trente et quarante" and "sept a lever"*, but I had been in communication with too many persons of late, to be ignorant that this little place was the rendezvous where a much deeper game than faro or rouge-et-noir was playing.

There were many persons at this time in the village from the States lying adjacent to the Mississippi, under the pretence of purchasing government lands, but whose real object was to encourage the settlers in Texas to throw off their allegiance to the Mexican government. Having nothing whatever in common with their plans, and no inclina-tion to forward or oppose them, I perceived that the longer I staid the more they would find reason to suppose I was a spy upon their ac-tions, and as soon as the Judge had spoken to a few of his friends we came away..."

* Games of chance.

Mr. Featherstonhaugh did a bit of thinking. He had made plans to visit the plantation of Dr. Isaac Newton Jones, on the south side of Red River, so the next morning he rode quickly through Washington, on down to Dooley's Ferry, and recorded in his Journal:

> It has occurred to me before I crossed Red River that it would be prudent not to prolong my stay in Texas at this time. All the persons I had had any intercourse with, appeared to be of one opinion as to the expediency and propriety of occupying and detaching that province from the Mexican government, and it was easy to see that they thought the moment for action was drawing nigh. Meanwhile, there was something to be seen here and I set about making the best use of the time I had...

He was conducted over the Jones plantation by the overseer on the following day and after admiring the enormous cotton bolls that reminded him of great white roses in bloom — and after philosophizing (privately, to his Journal) concerning the grave blunder the Mexicans had made in allowing the Americans to get a toehold in their country —

> I made a collection of such vines of the muscadel grape as I thought might be cultivated with success, and put them up with some other things in wet moss — and the last thing I did...was to cut myself a fine stick of the Bois d'Arc; then seating myself upon my faithful Missouri, amidst all sorts of bundles and sticks, I turned my back upon the fair and sunny fields of Texas, now doomed to the curse of slave labor, and on as serene, beautiful, and soft a December morning as ever was graced by a cloudless sky in Italy, I once more reached the banks of Red River...

And far to the southwest, in Mexico City, Stephen Austin is in prison; the new President of Mexico, Antonio Lopez de Santa Anna, had arrested him in December, 1833, when Stephen arrived in Mexico City with a petition from a second San Felipe Convention requesting that Texas be recognized as an independent state. Stephen Austin would remain in prison until July of 1835.

DAVY CROCKETT
COMES THROUGH WASHINGTON

November — 1835

IN NOVEMBER 1835, the great Tennessee hero, Davy Crockett, came down the Southwest Trail on his way to join Sam Houston's army in Texas.

What a week that was for the village!

The people all came in from the plantations, speeches were made from the courthouse steps, little boys threw their coonskin caps in the air and shouted "Huzzah!"

Everyone was laughing at the remark that Davy had made back in Tennessee a few weeks earlier when he was stumping for re-election to Congress. Davy had said, "If you re-elect me to Congress I will serve you faithfully; if you don't, you may go to the Devil and I will go to Texas!"

And here he was on his way to Texas. He had lost the election. "Old Hickory" hadn't liked him.

Davy himself laughed out loud at several remarks that he heard while he was in Washington. He had no more than arrived in town and stopped to water his horse at the town well, when the landlord of the tavern stepped up and said, "Good mornin' Mister — I don't rightly remember your name."

"It's of no consequence," Davy answered.

The landlord considered for a moment and said, "Seems to me I've seen you somewhere before."

"Very likely you have," Davy answered, "I've been there frequently."

A few more questions were asked by the landlord, a few more evasive answers given by Davy — all of which he faithfully recorded (so the story goes) in the journal he was keeping as he traveled.

After a few days of celebrating in the town, Davy and his half-dozen mounted companions rode down to the Red River and crossed at Dooley's Ferry. They galloped over the plains of Texas and as they crossed the edge of the field belonging to James and Isabella Clark, Isabella saddled her horse and rode after them. Comanches were on the warpath again, she warned them. They must change their course. Isabella turned them in a different direction and they, too, came to the plantation of Dr. Isaac Newton Jones where they spent a few days.

Then they were on their way to the Alamo.

CALENDAR OF EVENTS IN TEXAS IN 1836

Feb. 12, 1836: Davy Crockett & his party arrived at the Alamo. Col. James Bowie was there.

March 2, 1836: A convention met at Washington-On-The-Brazos where Texas made a formal Declaration of Independence from Mexico.

March 6, 1836: The Alamo fort was stormed by 3,000 Mexicans under General Santa Anna. All 188 men defending the fort were killed. As the bodies were piled in the courtyard to be burned, a Mexican soldier picked up a large knife with "J. Bowie" carved on one side of the hilt and the initials "J.B." carved on the other side.

April 21, 1836: Gen. Sam Houston and his army annihilated 1,600 Mexicans at San Jacinto, achieving the independence of Texas from Mexico.

Oct. 22, 1836: Gen Sam Houston was installed as the president of the Republic of Texas.

Dec. 27, 1836: Stephen F. Austin died in Austin, Texas, broken in body and spirit from his long imprisonment.

THE TERRITORY OF ARKANSAS BECOMES THE STATE OF ARKANSAS

1836

IN OCTOBER OF 1835 — one month before Davy Crockett came through Washington on his way to fight for Texas independence — the Ninth Territorial General Assembly met in Little Rock, and called for a convention to meet and frame a constitution as the basis for requesting that Arkansas be made a state of the Union.

The representatives from Hempstead County to the Ninth General Assembly were William Shaw and Hewitt Burt of Washington, and Dr. James Walker from the village of Columbus. The Secretary for the Council of the Ninth Assembly was Simon T. Sanders, of Washington. The Speaker of the House was Col. John Wilson, who had lived in the settlement of Hempstead Court House during the eight years in which he served as a representative from Hempstead County, and who had then moved to the Ouachita River where he promptly became a representative from Clark County.

The men of Washington dominated the political scene in the territorial capital of Little Rock. They arrived with their ruffled shirts and gold-headed canes and their wives came along in their silks and velvets.

Washington had become a town of lawyers. The little white frame law offices fronted every sandy street. And it seemed that as soon as a new young lawyer came to town and hung out his shingle he began immediately to go up in the world.

There was something magic about the hill!

William Trimble, who had come as the first prosecuting attorney in 1821, had risen to be a judge of the Circuit Court and then to become a judge of the Territorial Supreme Court.

Edward Cross, who had arrived as the first county land surveyor, had been appointed a judge of the Superior Court.

Thomas Hubbard, a young man from Connecticut, started his law practice in Washington in 1826, and by the time he was twenty-three he was known as Judge Hubbard, prosecuting attorney for the First Judicial District.

Another brilliant young lawyer, Daniel Ringo, opened a law practice in Washington in 1830 and soon he had been appointed a prosecuting attorney for the judicial circuit.

Grandison Royston of Tennessee, cousin to Zachary Taylor, had come riding into town in 1833 with his black man-servant John Dixon riding beside him, and within a year Grandison Royston was riding the trails and fording the streams as a prosecuting attorney with Hubbard and Ringo.

Two Conway cousins, William and George Conway, were starting their rise toward the state legislature from law offices in Washington, and another Trimble was coming — John Trimble — who would be appointed a judge of the Hempstead County Probate Court as soon as he arrived.

Two brothers from the east, Samuel and Bernard Hempstead, cousins to the Edward Hempstead of Missouri for whom Hempstead County was named — were beginning to thunder oratorically from the log courthouse — and the most dramatic speaker of them all, Albert Pike, of the long flowing locks and the penchant for poetry, who had a residence in Little Rock but kept a second law practice in Washington, could make the walls of the courthouse ring when he pleaded a case concerning the theft of one small pig with phrases from Tacitus, Homer and William Shakespeare.

The walls of the old log courthouse had become too small.

Tilman Patterson was appointed to build another courthouse.

In January 1836, the Constitutional Convention met in Little Rock with Col. John Wilson as the president, and Grandison Royston and Dr. James Walker as the delegates representing Hempstead County. A resolution was adopted at this convention that it was expedient to form a state constitution and a state government.

On April 14 — two weeks before the battle at San Jacinto which achieved Texas independence — the Senate of the United States adopted the bill that would admit Arkansas as a state of the Union. There had been much bitter debate over the question of slavery in the Arkansas Territory.

On June 15, President Andrew Jackson signed the bill that made ARKANSAS the TWENTY-FIFTH STATE OF THE UNITED STATES OF AMERICA.

The Arkansas Gazette carried great headlines:

GOD SAVE THE COMMONWEALTH OF ARKANSAS

LET ILLUMINATION BEGIN IN
EVERY HOUSE SIMULTANEOUSLY.

LET THERE BE RINGING OF THE TAVERN BELLS

ORATIONS

READING OF THE DECLARATION OF INDEPENDENCE

The little town of Washington was well represented when the first governor for the State of Arkansas was inaugurated on September 13, 1836. It was Grandison Royston who escorted Governor James Sevier Conway to the ceremony in the Senate chamber of the new State Capitol with the fluted columns which faced the Arkansas River in Little Rock.

Judge Daniel Ringo of Washington had been appointed Chief Justice of the Arkansas Supreme Court.

In a very short while Judge Edward Cross would be elected United States Representative from the new state of Arkansas.

WASHINGTON IN THE FIRST TEN YEARS
OF ARKANSAS STATEHOOD

1836 — 1846

THE SHOCKING NEWS REACHED Washington in early December of 1837 that one of its most esteemed former townsmen, Col. John Wilson, Speaker of the House of Representatives, had killed a colleague, Col. J.J. Anthony, with a bowie knife during an argument in the House chamber of the State Capitol in Little Rock.

Grandison Royston had tried to prevent the tragedy. As Col. Wilson advanced down the aisle toward Col. Anthony, his knife drawn, Grandison Royston leaped up from his seat on the aisle and thrust a chair between the two men. Col. Wilson had knocked the chair up with one hand, reached under it with the other hand, and plunged his knife into Col. Anthony's heart. Col. Anthony had died immediately on the floor of the House of Representatives.

Col. Wilson was expelled from the General Assembly. Grandison Royston was elected Speaker of the House in his stead.

The big news in Washington in 1838 was the moment when the first stagecoach appeared on the rise of the long hill beyond the Town Creek (the old Black Bois d'Arc creek) and came rumbling down over the bridge and up to the middle of town.

Now the travelers could be spared the long ride by horseback down the Southwest Trail. It took the stagecoach only thirty-eight hours to travel the hundred-and-twenty miles from Little Rock.

In 1839 the first issue of The Washington Telegraph came off the small printing press brought by William Etter by flatboat down the Mississippi from Pennsylvania.

There were ten stores in Washington now.

Abraham Block still owned the largest mercantile store on the hill. His two sons, Henry and Augustus, operated a Storage & Commission store in Fulton. They did a brisk business in slaves. The Blacks were arriving weekly on the steamboats that were able to easily navigate the Red River since Captain Shreve and his snagboats had managed to clear the river for seventy-five miles of the hazardous mass of log jams known as 'the great raft.'

When the steamboats went back downriver again they were jammed to the smokestacks with bale upon bale of cotton bound for the international port of New Orleans.

A town had been named for Captain Shreve fifty miles down river — Shreveport, Louisiana.

The Reverend William Stevenson came back to visit Washington in 1838 when the Arkansas Methodist District Conference met once more at the site of the old Ebenezer Camp Ground: "He was a tall old man, his locks were white, he had lost one eye; thin-visaged, he looked like a battle-scarred soldier who had seen service in the Army of the Lord a score of times and had returned after the smoke had passed away to review the fields his valor had won." — so wrote a visiting preacher to the conference.

There was no Methodist church building yet in Washington; the Methodist District Conference had to meet in the new white frame two-story courthouse that stood on the crown of the hill where the old log courthouse had been for a dozen years.

A Presbyterian minister was in town — the Rev. James Black, no relation at all to James Black, who had made the bowie knife in 1831. The Presbyterians had tried three times to organize a church; three times something happened to prevent it — the last time, the pastor named Alexander Banks had married Miss Elizabeth Pratt, school teacher from New York, and gone with her to open an academy for young ladies at the village of Spring Hill near Dooley's Ferry on Red River.

Wealthy men — quite wealthy men — had begun to emerge from the cotton plantations where once the first little settlements had appeared. Mound Prairie had become only farm lands. Columbus was a prosperous village. Fulton was a lusty river town. The area once known as Hempstead Court House was now called "Marlbrook", from the name given by Judge Edward Cross to his plantation on the Marlbrook Creek.

Many of the young men from the plantations were being sent away to schools on the other side of the Mississippi River; their sisters attended the Spring Hill Academy or other female academies in other southern states.

27

The small children of the plantations had their own schoolroom set up in a room in their own home, where a schoolmistress lived in as she taught. When these children reached the age where the schoolmistress could no longer handle them — or when the autumn rains made the roads so muddy that a fence rail had to be used to poke the thick black gumbo from the spokes of the wagon wheels — the family left the plantation in charge of the overseer for the winter and came into Washington. Here the children attended one of the two subscription schools set up east and west of the hill.

The schoolmaster, Daniel Witter, had served two terms in the territorial legislature and another term as sheriff of Hempstead County.

Some of the familiar faces have moved away. Judge Edward Cross and his Laura Frances left for Washington D.C. when he was elected U.S. Congressman. Judge Daniel Ringo moved to Little Rock to be near the bench of the Arkansas Supreme Court.

The home of James Black had been boarded up and sold. So had the home of his father-in-law William Shaw.

A great sorrow had come to James Black in 1838. Anne, his wife, had died, leaving him with four sons and a baby daughter, all under nine years of age.

William Shaw had never become reconciled to the marriage of his daughter to James Black. He brooded over Anne's tragedy.

According to the story of the town — one day, a year after Anne's death, William Shaw walked into the house where James Black lay ill with chills and fever and struck his son-in-law again and again with a heavy stick. William Shaw would have killed James Black, they said, if the family dog had not attacked him and driven him away.

James Black never recovered from the effects of that beating. A year later his eyes were still so inflamed from the blows to his head that he knew he was going blind.

But he had money. He could afford good medical treatment. He set out for Philadelphia where he knew there were good doctors in the hospital that Benjamin Franklin had founded. On the way he was sidetracked by a man on the riverboat who told him of a famous eye doctor in Cincinnati. This doctor proved to be a charlatan; the man on the boat had been his decoy. After months of treatment from the quack doctor in Cincinnati James Black's eyesight was worse than ever.

He went on to Philadelphia and received treatment there, but after several more months he started home to Arkansas by way of New Orleans, to consult an eye specialist there — and again the verdict was the same — they could do nothing to save his eyesight.

By the time James Black returned to his home in Washington he had been gone for two years. More sorrow was waiting for him there. William Shaw went to court and obtained guardianship of the five children. The proceeding can still be seen in the handwriting of the clerk for the autumn term of the probate court in 1841: "On this day William Shaw came into court and entered into indenture with Burkett D. Jett, Judge of the Probate Court of Hempstead County in the State of Arkansas for the children of James Black: viz: William Jefferson Black, Grandison Black, John Colbert Black, and Sydonham Black, males, until they respectively arrive at the age of twenty-one years, and Sarah Jane Black, female, until she arrives at the age of eighteen years."

At the spring term of court in 1842 William Shaw had liquidated all of James Black's holdings and had disappeared into Texas with the five children.

James Black had lost everything — his wife, his home, his blacksmith shop, and even if he had been able to keep his children he had nothing to offer them — his eyesight was almost gone and he had no means of livelihood.

Two friends offered him a home on their plantation near the Red River, but several months later he heard that Dr. Isaac Newton Jones had moved to Washington from his plantation on the other side of Red River and James Black came to consult with him. Was there anything that Dr. Jones could do to save his eyesight?

Dr. Jones tried. He let James Black live in the little office building at the corner of his property while he gave him treatments. At last Dr. Jones had to say that he could do nothing more.

James Black was forty-three years old in this year of 1842. He would live with the Jones family, with only interims with other town families when Dr. Jones was out of town, until he died in 1872. The children of the town would grow up calling him "Uncle Jimmy". They would come to stand in the doorway of the little office building and watch James Black set colored jewels in the handles of the few knives that he was able to make on the small forge which Dr. Jones had set up for him in the back yard.

ANOTHER RENDEZVOUS IN WASHINGTON

1846

N 1846 TEXAS HAD TO fight her war with Mexico all over again — only this time the whole of the United States was fighting with her and California had been added to the agenda.

General Santa Anna had come into power again in Mexico in 1842. In 1843 he had notified the government of the United States that the government of Mexico would consider it an open declaration of war if Texas was annexed as American territory — and on December 8, 1845, the United States had formally declared Texas to be a state of the Union.

On the last day of April, 1846, the first Mexican army crossed the Rio Grande and laid siege to Fort Texas.

President James Polk proclaimed a Declaration of War between the United States and the Republic of Mexico. Governor Drew, of Arkansas, issued a call for one regiment of cavalry, and one battalion of five companies of infantry, to volunteer for one year of service in the War with Mexico.

Washington was designated as the rendezvous point for the volunteers to be enrolled and mustered into service.

On June 22, the first soldiers who had volunteered for the Mexican War rode into Washington from Sevier County. They rode on out to the spring two miles east of town where one of the 'stands' had been when the Choctaw and Chickasaw Indians made their march. The stand was a Baptist camp meeting ground now; the stone basin of the baptistry by the spring was used as a watering trough for the horses.

On the same day of June 22, four of the companies for the Arkansas Regiment of Cavalry left Little Rock to march toward Washington. "It was a proud sight for our citizens," wrote one bystander, "to behold column after column of these daring and noble spirits sweep by and gallantly debouch upon the Military Road...."

By July 10, all ten companies had been mustered into service, and old Nick Trammell, notorious highwayman, had been sent for to lead the way into Mexico. He knew every trail.

Over the rise of the long hill beyond the Town Creek came column after column of the men on the way to San Antonio — over the bridge and up the hill, on past the crossroads and down through the hollow. Many of the young men of the town were marching away with them as the lines of cavalry and artillery and infantry disappeared in clouds of dust from the Southwest Trail.

And this was only the beginning.

In August the volunteers from Tennessee were encamped at the spring two miles east of town, waiting to be enrolled for the War with Mexico. When the Tennessee volunteers had marched down the road to the ferries on Red River it was time for the volunteers from Kentucky to come through. All during the summer and autumn months the men on their way to fight in Mexico were encamped in and around Washington. One company of infantry had to camp on the Prairie de Roane, eight miles south of town, where the boys from Washington hauled water to them by oxcart.

Then it was winter and the time for waiting.

During the winter of 1846-1847 the first Female Academy was built in Washington. Work was commenced on the Male Academy. A Temperance Society was organized in the Methodist Church with twenty-eight members taking THE PLEDGE OF TOTAL ABSTINENCE.

Judge Thomas Hubbard, who had remained a bachelor all these years, married the widow Barbara Garland who had lived in the town of Spring Hill for the past few years with her two sons — Rufus, aged fourteen and Augustus, aged twelve.

Abraham Block ran a notice in The Washington Telegraph:

> The undersigned having this day associated with himself in business his sons, DAVID BLOCK and VIRGINIUS BLOCK, the business hereafter will be conducted under the style of A. BLOCK AND SONS.

Also, in The Washington Telegraph:

> MARRIED: In this place on the 22nd inst. by the Rev. Lively, William W. Andrews, Esq., to Miss Elizabeth L., daughter of Dr. Isaac N. Jones.

Editor Etter complained about the mail service without mentioning any names. (His neighbor, Elias Carruth, had charge of the tri-weekly mail service from Shreveport on the south, to Fort Towson on the west.)

LOST MAIL: The mail from Ft. Towson eastward was lost in the Cossatot again on Friday last. The rider says he attempted to ford the stream, but that it proved to be swimming, and that his horse was swept down by the current and it was with much difficulty that he saved himself and horse. The mail, he says, was a small one and probably contained but little of value.

Then, on May 27, 1847:

RETURN OF OUR VOLUNTEERS: The time is at hand when the volunteers from this State will leave the toils and privations of the war in Mexico for the comforts and enjoyments of home. Too late to take part in the storming of Monterey, anxious for an encounter with the enemy, fearful that the war would be brought to a close and they be sent home without an opportunity of distinguishing themselves, their anxiety was relieved and their fears dispelled by the appearance of a Mexican army under Santa Anna at Buena Vista....

On June 14, the Washington Telegraph printed headlines:

IMPORTANT FROM MEXICO

PEACE!!   PEACE!!   PEACE!!

But Editor Etter was mistaken — that report was nothing more than wishful thinking brought up the Southwest Trail by one of the first volunteers to return from his year of service. Peace would not come until after September 14, when Mexico City would be captured and the flag of the United States raised by a battalion of U.S. Marines over "the halls of Montezumo."

In the meantime, all those columns of cavalry and infantry and artillery had to come marching back up the Southwest Trail, on through Washington and on toward Little Rock and over the Mississippi River to Kentucky and Tennessee. "They are generally well," reported the Washington Telegraph, "and in their bronzed faces and strengthened forms have evident signs of long and arduous service. Several of Captain Pike's company, resident amongst us, have returned."

Not all have returned: Adjt. E.M. Vaughan and Capt. E.J. Alexander had fallen at Buena Vista.

On March 10, 1848 the Treaty of Guadalupe Hidalgo was ratified by the United States Senate, which confirmed American possession of Texas, of California, of New Mexico, of Oregon.

In the same week a small notice appeared in The Washington Telegraph:

The Rev. James Black, we are requested to state, will preach the funeral sermon of the late Elijah Stuart on Sunday next at 11 a.m..

Elijah Stuart was the man who had set the first house and tavern on the hill of the five trails twenty-five years ago.

An era had passed.

THE ANTE-BELLUM YEARS

1849 — 1860

OW THE MURPHY wagons that creaked up the hill, and the stagecoaches that rumbled over the bridge of the Town Creek, were beginning to wear the road down. The hill was made of sand!

Gold had been found out there in California. One of the roads to the gold fields came "by way of the old Spanish Trail that leads to Santa Fe through the Red River Valley and Texas" and the Army of '49 was singing as it came:

> The pilot bread is in my mouth
> The gold dust in my eye
> I'm bound for Californ-yia
> Susannah, don't you cry!

Day after day the wagons rolled through Washington; sometimes they had to camp for a week on the banks of the Red River, waiting their turn to be poled across.

The years following the War with Mexico were golden years for life around the hill, too. Cotton was king! The plantations were prosperous. There were buggies and carriages in the streets of Washington and dinner lists in the hotels, with wines from the east.

Soon there were five hotels in town (the taverns had become saloons.) Traveling theatrical troups came to play in the courthouse and there was talk of building an opera house.

Advertisements for the store of Brittin & Andrews bespoke:

BIG NEWS!! BIG NEWS!!

Just received from New York, Boston and New Orleans, an extensive and well selected stock of DRY GOODS.

GENTS CLOTHING: COATS - sup'r French black cloth coats. Do do paletots. PANTS - Sup'r French black cashmere, doeskin, French cassimere.

VESTS: Black satin, roling and standing collar. Figur'd satin, embroidered linen and white Marseilles. Linen bosom shirts.

FOR THE LADIES: French ivory fans, French kid boots, Valenciennes lace, corsets, doeskin gloves, watered silk, mousseline de soie...

The second generation had come of age on the hill. The older sons had fought in the Mexican War while the younger sons clerked in their fathers' stores, or read law, or finished their schooling on the other side of the Mississippi, and now they all began to marry "the girl next door."

There were fox hunts in the moonlight. There were formal-dress balls in the houses on the plantations — more balls in the houses in Washington — there were hoopskirts and candlelight, shining silver dishes on the rosewood and mahogany sideboards, and the song of the mockingbird in the crepe myrtle bushes around the doorways.

The new houses built in Washington at this time were small, of Greek Revival architecture. It was the big house out on the plantation that had tall columns at the front and the winding carriage drive past the magnolia and catalpa trees that had been planted among the pines and oaks.

Grandison Royston had gone out one day with a pocketful of magnolia seeds and planted magnolia trees in the yards of his neighbors. One magnolia tree that he planted in the front yard of the Isaac Newton Jones' home in 1839, when Daniel Webster Jones was six months old, was growing tall — and so was Daniel Webster Jones.

James Black still made a few things in copper and brass at his forge behind the home of Dr. Isaac Newton Jones. Little boys were told to go pump the bellows for the forge when they were too much underfoot. "Go on over and visit with Uncle Jimmy," their mothers would say, "He's a lonely old man and he needs company."

Some of the wealthier families made trips to the east now and then. They would board the stagecoach at the livery stable in the middle of town and be gone for months at a time.

When Pauline Gratiot married Major Bernard Hempstead they traveled to New York for their honeymoon and made a boat trip up the Hudson River. Here they visited at the home of the novelist, Washington Irving, where he gave them clippings of the ivy from the stone walls around his home and told them that the first clippings had come from the castle of Sir Walter Scott, in Scotland. Pauline Hempstead brought the ivy clippings back with her and planted them around her new home on the outskirts of Washington. Soon it became a tradition to give a clipping of Sir Walter Scott's ivy as a marriage blessing to every new bride in town.

There were many new brides in Washington. Everyone had become a matchmaker. When Grandison Royston was talking with a colleague, Harris Flanagin, in the legislative chambers in Little Rock one day, he chided Mr. Flanagin for still being a bachelor. "I know the wife for you," Grandison Royston said, "Her name is Martha Nash and she lives in Washington."

35

The next day Harris Flanagin saddled his horse and rode down the Southwest Trail to Washington. He knocked on the door of the Nash home; he presented his credentials and asked permission to court Martha. The family asked him to dine with them that evening. At nine o'clock he proposed. He was accepted. Three weeks later there was a fabulous wedding with several slaves as a marriage portion. (Martha Nash Flanagin's husband would be the governor of Arkansas in a few more years.)

Then there was the trip East that Simon Sanders, Clerk of the Hempstead County Court, made when he decided that his two daughters, Virginia, aged sixteen, and Zenobia, aged fourteen, needed to see more of the world. They stopped off in Culpepper county, Virginia, to visit a sister of Mrs. Sanders — Mrs. Albert Gallatin Simms — and when the Sanders family returned to Washington the girls brought their cousin Zenobia Simms to spend the winter.

Now there was even more of a social life around the hill. There were many Sanders cousins in the area. Mrs. Sanders had another sister in Washington, Mrs. Ephraim Mirick — and another sister had been the first wife of Dr. Robert Walker at the town of Columbus — so there were balls in the plantation home of the Walkers at Columbus, and musicales in the parlor of the Mirick home out on the Southwest Trail, and literary readings in the library of the Sanders home in Washington.

In February of 1852 there was a double wedding: Zenobia Simms of Virginia married Robert Walker of Columbus — and Isabelle Walker married Rufus Garland, son of Judge and Mrs. Thomas Hubbard of Washington.

The two young daughters of Simon T. Sanders were the attendants for their cousin Zenobia Simms; Augustus Garland was the best man for his brother Rufus. Within a year Augustus Garland, not quite twenty-one, had married Virginia Sanders, not quite eighteen. (Virginia Sanders' husband would become a governor of Arkansas in quite a few more years.)

But to pause for a moment at the year 1852.

There was not a foot of railroad track west of the Mississippi at this time. In 1852 the Cairo & Fulton Railroad was incorporated, with Daniel Ringo as vice-president, and Edward Cross as one of the promoters. A preliminary survey was made for the railroad to come from Cairo, Illinois, to Fulton on Red River, with the line of the tracks to follow the line of the Southwest Trail.

36

Nothing happened for a few years and then it was time for the War Between the States.

During those next few years the Presbyterian Church flourished at last in Washington. The church building was raised in the middle of town and the Rev. Samuel Williamson, president of Davidson College in North Carolina, came as pastor at a salary of $800 per annum.

The Temperance Society flourished in a different way. The Society had persuaded the township to abolish the retailing of spiritous liquors in quantities of less than a quart, and Peter Cox sent for the carpenter Henry Cheatham to set up a Blind Tiger in his saloon. The bar was boarded up leaving one hole with a revolving wheel behind it that had narrow compartments labeled "Whisky Straight" "Whisky Toddy" etc. By placing a dime in the compartment of his choice the customer could turn the revolving wheel, the proper drink would appear, and Peter Cox told his friends that neighbors who had never taken a drink before in their lives became so fascinated with his innovation that his profits doubled.

On still nights the lonesome sound of the steamboat whistle could be heard from the Red River. Bale after bale of cotton was going downriver to New Orleans.

Everyone owned cottonfields: almost everyone owned slaves.

Now and then one of the trusted young female house slaves would be sent to New Orleans by way of one of the steamboats to attend a special school where she would be taught the art of hairdressing, or of dressmaking, or the secrets of fine French cooking.

Out on the plantation of Capt. Matthew Moss there was an old old black man with an interesting story; he had wandered into town one day, saying that his name was Stephen Washington, and he had been a body servant to George Washington during the Revolutionary War. Capt. Moss had taken the ancient one in and made him the overseer of his slaves.

On the plantation of David Block there was a young black man with an even wilder tale to tell — his ancestor had come with Hernando de Soto on that first exploring party through Arkansas in 1541!

This ancestor, said young Bob Samuels, had been one of the fortunate few who had returned to Spain after that adventure. Then, several generations later, another ancestor had joined another party of adventurers coming to America, and when they reached Gaines Landing on the

37

Mississippi River they had hired Nicholas Trammell to lead them into Mexico. Somewhere in the province of Texas, Nick Trammell had murdered the men and taken the women into slavery. The woman who became Bob Samuels' grandmother had been forced to marry a half-breed Mexican, or Indian, or Black — and a generation later, when Nick Trammell moved to Texas, he sold Becca, the mother, and her children, Bob, aged 1, and Mary, aged 4, to Abraham and David Block.

Many new white faces had come to the hill.

Thomas Simms, aged eighteen, had come from Virginia to visit his sister, Mrs. Zenobia Simms Walker, and had decided to stay. He sent for his brother Montcalm to visit, and Montcalm decided to stay. They sent for their parents to visit — Mr. and Mrs. Albert Gallatin Simms — and they decided to stay.

Henry Moses of Virginia came at the same time with his bride Susan Raleigh, a direct descendant of Sir Walter Raleigh.

A few Hatfields came from Tennessee, but the McCoys went right on down the Trail and into Texas.

John Eakin opened a law practice in Washington; he was a Yale man, a Greek and Latin scholar. His brother-in-law Alchyny Delony followed — another Greek and Latin scholar.

Five young Carrigan brothers arrived in two long journeys from North Carolina. Alfred Carrigan, newly graduated from the University at Chapel Hill, had come first on an exploring trip and purchased acres and acres of land for himself, his father, his brothers, his aunts and uncles and cousins.

Sixty-thousand dollars in gold came in two big black iron washpots in those nine-week journeys from North Carolina. The gold had been placed in the bottom of the pots, cottonseed tucked over the gold, blankets tucked around the cottonseed, and the little babies of the slaves placed in their cradles of the big black pots as they jounced over the Wilderness Road through the Cumberland Gap and down the Southwest Trail into Washington.

Now there were Holts and Carruths and Bensons and Bookers and Martins and Monroes and Shields and Jetts and Duggers and Greens in the cotton plantations that stretched far around the hill and south into the canebrakes of the Prairie de Roane where once only bears and panthers roamed.

Everybody was beginning to be related to everybody else.

In one of the very first family caravans to come by pack mules down the Southwest Trail into Southwest Arkansas in 1814 there had been a Clark married to a Stuart. Then the Clarks and Stuarts had married Fontaines; the Clarks and Stuarts and Fontaines married Smiths and Cheathams and Johnsons and Hills — and the black slaves took the names of their white masters so that the black Johnsons married the black Cheathams, and the black Cheathams and Johnsons married the black Stuarts and Conways and Greens and Walkers —

And everybody — black and white — was raising everybody's children.

On Sundays, when the families attended services in the Baptist church with the four pillars squared from four great pines, or the Methodist church with the tall spire, or the Presbyterian church with the hand-carved pews, or the Grace Episcopal Church with the golden cross — the black slaves sat in the balconies with the little children of their white masters, and there was a special time in the service for the special song of the slaves, called a "spiritual" — which was all part of that greater picture of the receipt which would pass from one white hand to another bearing the words, "Received . . . one thousand and fifty dollars for Henry, Negro boy, sound, sensible, and healthy and a slave for life."

It was 1860.

The main street of Washington was called Franklin Street; it was nothing more than the old Southwest Trail become town-conscious. A few of the oldtimers with long white beards would be seen there occasionally, tapping their canes on the boardwalk as they walked to the courthouse to pay their taxes, or offering an arm to a pretty granddaughter of one of their old friends when she needed help across the sandy street.

Judge Edward Cross had retired after three terms in Congress and several years as Associate Justice of the Arkansas Supreme Court.

Judge Daniel Witter had retired from his long tenure as County Judge.

Dr. Nathan Smith took down his physician's sign and retired to his farm where he had built the circle of little cabins to serve as the first hospital in Hempstead County. Dr. Smith had become the first "weatherman" for Arkansas; for the past twenty years he had kept a journal of weather conditions on his farm where the mulberry trees were growing for cultivation of silkworms, and in 1859 the newly-founded

Smithsonian Institute in Washington D.C. asked to publish his Meteorological Observations. The Institute sent him blanks to fill out. Dr. Smith answered:

> Secretary of the Smithsonian Institute
> Dear Sir:
>   The blanks I have lately received from the Institution I shall only be able to fill up in the manner I have done during the last few months; nor can I make observations at night, for myself and family always retire before 9 o'clock. I live on my little farm, three miles out from Washington, supported by the personal labor of my children, on the farm I scooped out for them from the forest, so many years ago. I am necessarily at leisure, for I am in my sixty-ninth year.

As for the field of politics, Washington was still proving to be a star-crossed hill for young lawyers. Alfred Carrigan was sitting in the senate of the Twelfth General Assembly. Rufus Garland had represented Hempstead County in the state legislature; so had his younger brother Augustus Garland.

The little town would outdo herself in this last year of the antebellum days. One of her youngest lawyers, Edward Gantt, would be elected United States Representative from Arkansas. One of her elder politicians, Dr. Charles Mitchel, would be elected United States Senator.

THE DAYS OF SECESSION

1860 — 1861

*T*HE PRINTING OFFICE of The Washington Telegraph was located in a long narrow two-story building on Franklin Street in Washington. William Etter had bought the building in 1852 and made a home in it for his printing press as well as for his wife and four sons and two daughters.

John Eakin, lawyer, became the editor of The Washington Telegraph in 1860.

There was also a printer's devil living in the Etter home — Sam Williams — who would go with The Chicago Tribune after the Civil War, and write his **Memorabilia of Hempstead County** in 1886, but on a November day in 1860 he was alone in the office of The Washington Telegraph. He wrote of that day many years later:

> The day following the presidential election day was an uncommonly gloomy one for November. It was ushered in with rain, and all day long there had been a constant downpour. As I sat alone by the window and gazed out upon the dark pall of clouds that enveloped the earth, and listened to the ceaseless patter of the rain, I felt a vivid presentiment that the forbidding scene was a presage of the dreadful feeling of gloom that was about to be cast over the entire South by the news of Lincoln's election.
>
> In due course of time — I think it was the third day — intelligence of the result reached Washington. Abraham Lincoln had been chosen! The announcement fell upon our little community with the awfulness of a death knell. The entire male population assembled at the post office before the arrival of the stagecoach, and when the intelligence was given out a feeling of sadness fell over us: with leaden hearts the little knots of men finally dispersed to their homes ...

Abraham Lincoln was the man who, when he had been elected senator from Illinois two years earlier, had said, "I believe that this government cannot endure permanently half slave and half free..."

Lincoln was the man who, when he was nominated for President of the United States, had campaigned on the Republican Platform which "condemned attempts to reopen the African slave trade and denied the authority of Congress to give legal status to slavery in the territories."

"States' rights!" — that was what the slaveholding states had always been shouting about — "States' rights! The federal government is only an agent of the states, and possesses no power except that which has been given it by the states themselves —"

41

But the War Between The States was here and it had come a few short months after that November presidential election day with a shot fired on Fort Sumter, in South Carolina, on April 12, 1861. Seven southern states had seceded from the United States of America and had demanded that the arsenal at Fort Sumter be delivered by the federal forces to the newly-formed Confederate States of America.

The moment of decision for Arkansas came when Simon Cameron, Secretary of War, sent a message to Governor Henry M. Rector, requisitioning "one regiment of 780 men to help suppress the rebellion..."

Governor Rector replied, "In answer to your demand for troops from Arkansas to subjugate the southern states, I have to say that none will be furnished."

A Secession Convention had been meeting in Little Rock at the time, to decide whether Arkansas should secede from the Union, and on May 2, the vote was taken. There were sixty-nine "ayes" and one "nay."

Arkansas seceded from the United States of America and accepted the provisional constitution of the Confederate States of America.

CIVIL WAR
1861 — 1865

NOTHING HAD REALLY prepared Washington for what was to come. The march of the Indians and the march of the men to the War with Mexico were nothing compared to the marches that would come and go on the Southwest Trail before the next four years were done.

In the beginning it was a gay lark. The war would not last long. They would go — the young men of the town — and they would show those Yankees from Yankeedoodle-dom a thing or two!

Then they would come home and everything would be the same as before.

Their first battle as a hometown unit was in August 1861, at Wilson's Creek in Missouri — not very far away — only a few hundred miles up the Southwest Trail, where so many of their grandparents had come from almost fifty years ago.

It was a terrible battle.

The young men had been so beautiful when they went marching over the Town Creek and up the Southwest Trail. Their luggage had followed them, in many carts, and most of the young men took their faithful black manservant along to keep their boots polished and their clothes brushed and in good order.

It was a terrible battle at Wilson's Creek!

They killed John Carrigan. They killed Montcalm Simms. Montcalm was found dead on the battlefield with his head resting on a flat gray stone. John Carrigan's father and Montcalm Simms' father drove in a wagon all the way to Missouri to bring their sons home. They brought back the bloodstained stone and placed it at the head of the grave in the new cemetery that the Presbyterians had set in the bend of the road beyond the tavern.

Two other hometown boys had been brought back and buried in that new cemetery — Billy Worsham and William Langston.

Thomas Simms was still alive but he had been shot almost to pieces. So had Homer Cross —

But the Confederate flag had been brought back without any dirt on it, thank God! The boys had not allowed it to touch the dust!

The company of the Hempstead Rifles was reorganized and twenty more young men rode away with their luggage and their manservants. They rode right back up toward Missouri, too. They had sent those Yankees scattering once. Let them dare to come back and try to set one foot over that line into Arkansas!

Most of the other young men in the town had already crossed the Mississippi to "smack the bluecoats good" over there.

This war would be over in time for spring planting.

By springtime the Yankees were trampling all over Missouri. Rufus Garland wrote a letter from camp in the northern mountains of Arkansas: "Tell the matrons and daughters not to be alarmed, they are safe. The enemy can never get down there although they have already come farther than they should have been allowed. But tell the boys to come out, we may need all the help we can get —"

There were not many boys left to come out. It was the middle-aged men who were closing the doors of their stores and offices and posting a notice: "Jas R. Page, Esq., will transact all my legal business until I will return."

A calvary company named "The Worsham Avengers" came galloping in from Lafayette County. They stayed in town long enough to be presented a banner by one of the young ladies; then they galloped on over the bridge and up the Southwest Trail toward Missouri.

There was another terrible battle at Elkhorn Tavern, four miles inside the Arkansas line, but no hometown boys were killed and Capt. Ed Jett wrote: "General Van Dorn says he is not whipped and that he cannot be whipped. We whipped them the first day and would have whipped them the second if we had one more hour before dark..."

Things were gloomy on the other side of the Mississippi. Kentucky had been abandoned by the graycoats — "..the heel of the invader is upon the neck of our beloved Tennessee...."

The Mississippi River had been blockaded down at New Orleans and there were no medicines in Washington to combat the measles and congestive fevers that were killing the little children and the oldtimers and even the brave boys from Texas as they came up the road on their way to Little Rock to enlist.

There was no thread to sew the uniforms for the soldiers. There was plenty of woolen and cotton material, but no spun thread —

Would everyone, everywhere, be willing to look the other way if we offered to exchange cotton with the enemy in return for medicines and other necessaries? No?

Then burn all the cotton on the docks along the Mississippi! Hide the rest of it! Do not allow a single bale of cotton to go southward on the Red River where it could fall into the hands of the enemy. Store it under huge sheds and keep it twenty miles back from any navigable stream.

But if we sell no cotton in the international port at New Orleans — and if the Yankees think they have to capture every bale they get — where do we get any money?

We'll make our own money! The government of the Confederate States of America is ready to go into operation over there in the capital of Richmond, Virginia, and we can print our own Confederate money. An exchange can be set up right here in Washington. We can have little paper coupons called "shinplasters" (because they are only large enough to plaster a skinned shin) and everybody can still be rich.

There is another terrible battle up in the northeast mountains at a place called Prairie Grove.

There is another terrible battle on the other side of the Mississippi at Corinth.

For six months the Yankees have been tunnelling, and sending gunboats up the Mississippi, trying to capture the last two river ports of Vicksburg and Port Hudson. Ten men from Hempstead County captured one of those gunboats — the PETROL — Privates A.D. Monroe and B.B. Chism brought back the flag.

Col. Henry Johnson was mortally wounded while leading his men in the gallant charge over the breastworks at Corinth —

If only so many of the sons and fathers were not dying so far away from home, where they cannot be brought back and buried by the side of their grandfathers. The faithful black manservant comes riding in with the gold watch, the shaving mug, the little folding mirror --

Then it was July of 1863. Vicksburg had fallen. Port Hudson had fallen. The entire length of the Mississippi River belonged to the enemy. General Frederick Steele with a Federal army of 9,000 men stood waiting on the Arkansas side of the Mississippi River, at Helena, for a column of

Federal cavalry to join them from the direction of the old road to Batesville. Then they would march toward Little Rock.

Up in the northern mountains the Federal forces of General Blount were pushing the Confederate troops of General Cabell down toward the Arkansas River.

General Kirby Smith, in command of the Trans-Mississippi armies of Arkansas, Texas, Louisiana, and the boys still fighting for Missouri, issued a message TO THE PEOPLE OF ARKANSAS: "The time has come for every man in his place, and as best he may, to do his whole duty. Do not entertain the idea that this State is to be given up to the enemy. It is not."

On September 10 General Frederick Steele and his augmented army of 13,500 men had marched across the prairies from Helena and captured Little Rock.

There was nowhere for anyone to go now but down into the southwest corner of Arkansas.

The war had just begun for Washington

The carts and wagons and carriages had started to appear over the rise of the long hill beyond the Town Creek during the hot month of July. A mother or grandmother would be driving the team, a small boy or two walking barefoot in the dust, the little children peering from the crannies of the bedding and household articles that had been piled in the vehicles.

They arrived with favorite rocking chairs and family Bibles but with very little clothing, and no food.

Many of the refugees had been refugees in Little Rock the winter before, after their homes in the northern part of the state had been ravaged and pillaged by the armies and renegade bands of "jayhawkers."

By the time of September, when General Steele entered Little Rock, the houses on the hill of Washington, and the houses on the plantations and all the villages around, had filled their spare rooms and attics with women and children. When the spare rooms and attics were filled, the few empty slave houses were used.

Still the refugees came down the Southwest Trail.

Lofts of the barns were cleared out and made into bedrooms; tents were put up out on the plantations and in the yards of the town houses.

By November it was obvious that with the late rains making the roads almost impassable with mud, no Federal troops were going to come down the Southwest Trail if they had any sense; a wagon could stick so tight in the thick black gumbo that it could take four oxen and four men with fence rails to pry it out again.

Washington felt safe; the whole Trans-Mississippi division of the Confederate army was between it and Little Rock. The army, too, had come down that road as General Steele entered Little Rock, and had spread out to various towns along the route.

General Sterling Price had set up the Arkansas headquarters for the Trans-Mississippi District in Camden, on the Ouachita River. The headquarters of the commander, General Kirby Smith, was in Shreveport, Louisiana, where he had called together the four governors of the four states to map future strategy. The west side of the Mississippi River was fighting alone now. There was no communication with the Confederate government in Richmond.

Washington settled in and held a ball. Davy Crockett's grandson was in town; so were Albert Pike's two lovely daughters and it seemed a good excuse to extend the hospitality of Washington again. Young ladies appeared in ball gowns that had not been worn in two years, and their partners were handsome young soldiers with shining brass buttons on their gray uniforms.

Soldiers were everywhere! Washington had become the "Post of Washington." Acres of tents had appeared where there had been acres of cottonfields.

Generals were everywhere! General Tom Dockery had his headquarters at the Moss plantation, between Washington and Fulton. General Cabell's headquarters were in Columbus, with his 3,000 men. General Marmaduke was at the Jones Hotel in Washington. General Evander MacNair's headquarters were in his own home in Washington. Out near Blevins was the encampment of old Jo Shelby, from where he and his daring raiders made forays to harass the enemy, all the way up into the northern mountains, across into Missouri and home again.

General Kirby Smith rode up the road from Shreveport to inspect the fortifications being built at Dooley's ferry and at Fulton on Red River. Everyone knew the Federals would start up the river in the springtime. General Kirby Smith came on up the Southwest Trail into Washington to inspect the breastworks being built along the Town Creek: everyone knew that General Steele would start down the Southwest Trail in the springtime. Then General Kirby Smith rode southeast to Camden, down the road that John Johnson had cut out so long ago, and held a conference with General Sterling Price.

Governor Harris Flanagin was living at the Oxley home on the southern edge of town. He had been called from a battlefield in Tennessee in the early days of the war to become the governor of the Confederate State of Arkansas.

Washington had become the capital for the Confederate State of Arkansas. All the government archives and all the government officials had come down the road from Little Rock as General Steele approached.

All the courts for the state, all the courts for Hempstead County and all the military courts were held in the small square courthouse on the crown of the hill.

Every law office, every little office building in the corner of the yards, had become a headquarters for military personnel. The Produce Loan Office was in Washington, the Quartermaster for the Clothing Bureau, the headquarters for Paroled and Exchanged Prisoners. All the veterans of the battles of Wilson's Creek and Elkhorn Tavern and Vicksburg and Port Hudson, who had been paroled or sent home on sick leave, had been issued orders to reorganize with their regimental, battalion, and company commanders at the Post of Washington.

It was the coldest December that Washington had ever known.

Snow fell on the acres of tents of the soldiers, and where women and children were setting up housekeeping with their favorite rocking chairs and family treasures.

Editor John Eakin, in the office of The Washington Telegraph, looked for his copy of Dr. Nathan Smith's Meteorological Observations which the Smithsonian Institute had published, so he could compare thermometer readings, but he couldn't find his copy. Dr. Smith sent him another with a note: "Dear Sir: I send you another copy of my Meteorological Observations, hoping you will be more careful with this. Last Friday was the coldest day I have recorded: the thermometer at sunrise stood at six degrees below zero. It is too cold to write more at present. Your friend, N. Smith."

The winter went by and the false spring of February came. Daffodils bloomed on the hillsides.

Arkansas had become a state divided. Two state governments were operating. In Little Rock, where the citizens had been required to take an Amnesty Oath, General Steele had set up a Federal government with Isaac Murphy as governor — the one man who had voted "Nay" when the vote had been taken for secession.

General Steele sent word to Washington that the state archives must be returned to Little Rock.

"This is about the coolest piece of impudence we have received," wrote John Eakin, in The Washington Telegraph. "Gen. Steele kindly urges our State officials to send the archives back, as they can no longer be of use to us. Messieurs Cunningham and Flanagin — pay attention!"

The answer, of course, was to go right on functioning as the Confederate State of Arkansas in the capital at Washington.

Another answer was to build up more brush and wire along the creeks and ravines; the spring rains had not come and the earth of the Southwest Trail was dry and hard.

It was March.

There were two things in Washington that the Federals wanted — the state archives and those bales of cotton that had been stored under huge sheds twenty miles back from any navigable stream.

In the March 16 issue of the newspaper John Eakin pointed out that The Washington Telegraph was the only rebel newspaper still publishing in the state; it had not missed an issue. The Arkansas Gazette, in Little Rock, had a Yankee publisher; William Woodruff, who had founded the newspaper in 1819, had been banished from the city with his four unmarried daughters, for refusing to take the Amnesty Oath.

"Very well," wrote Editor Eakin in The Washington Telegraph, "Let it be! He, Woodruff, comes to us like Wolsey, his grey hairs in the wind, and his helpless daughters around him. Whose turn next, we wonder?"

It was Editor Eakin's turn next. Suddenly no newspaper was printed in Washington for the entire month of April.

On May 11, the next copy of The Washington Telegraph appeared — and again it came from the office building on Franklin street in Washington, but for six weeks the type and press had been hidden in a barn on the south side of the Red River. Editor Eakin explained: "The temporary suspension of this journal was caused by the removal of the

49

press and type to a place of safety, on the approach of Gen. Steele's army.''

In March, General Ulysses S. Grant had sent word across the Mississippi for the Red River Campaign to begin. General Frederick Steele with approximately 8,000 men, 500 wagons, 16 pieces of artillery, 8,000 cavalry and draft animals, started his march down the Southwest Trail toward Washington.

At the same time General Nathaniel Banks had been ordered to proceed up Red River and take Shreveport, Louisiana. The Federals would recover the state archives, the hidden cotton would be captured, and the Confederacy would be crushed between the two armies. The road to Texas would be clear.

The Federals never made it.

General Steele left with his army from Little Rock and the rains came. Forty days later, he and the remnants of his wagons and mules, with his men so exhausted that they fell in the mud and slept where they lay — forty days later, General Steele was back in Little Rock and he never came down the Southwest Trail again. To him, it must have rained the entire forty days and forty nights.

General Nathaniel Banks' army had been destroyed on the Red River. For the first time in many years the waters had not risen high in the banks and Federal gunboats could not get through.

How jubilantly John Eakin could write in that May 11 issue of The Washington Telegraph. "All will be well! Do you not see that it will? Where is the strength of the North? Why was Banks cut to pieces in Louisiana and Steele disgracefully routed and chased to his base of operations in Little Rock?''

Nonetheless, the Yankees had come within eight miles of Washington. A scouting party had slipped in by one of the creeks and been captured in the deep ravine in front of the Dan Jones house — the prisoners had been chained in Judge Witter's old home.

Then Governor Flanagin with the state archives in a wagon, and John Eakin with the newspaper press and types in another wagon, had fled across the Red River to the little town of Rondo.

The rest of Washington sat and waited. At last they heard what happened.

General Steele and his men had reached Arkadelphia, on the Ouachita River crossing, with no opposition; they had crossed the Little

Missouri River after being joined by General Thayer coming from the northern mountains with 5,000 men, 300 wagons, 14 pieces of artillery — and all at once there was old Jo Shelby and his raiders behind them, and General Cabell and his men in front of them, and General Greene's men and General MacNair's men to the sides — striking like hornets, shrieking their rebel yell, disappearing into the underbrush, turning up somewhere else —

General Steele turned aside from the Southwest Trail and cut across the Prairie d'Ann to pick up the old Camden road that came from Washington. The Confederates were there again, skirmishing and disappearing. General Steele decided that it was Camden he wanted to capture, not Washington, and after a small but bloody battle on the Prairie d'Ann, the entire Federal army turned down the road in the direction of Camden and entered an empty city there on April 15.

The Rebels would not let the Federals stay in Camden either. There was no food left for them, and there was no forage for the animals. When the wagon trains were sent to plunder the outlying farms for supplies, old Jo Shelby was waiting for them again, and so was Sterling Price and Marmaduke and Fagan and all the boys —

General Steele and his half-starved army marched out of Camden, and arrived back in Little Rock in a rainstorm on May 3.

The wounded left behind on the Prairie d'Ann had been brought into Washington. Every building and every home became a hospital. Dr. Nathan Smith came from his farm to care for the wounded in the Baptist church. The weather had turned bitter cold again, with the woods so wet that no firewood could be found, and one of the pine pillars of the Baptist church was taken down and split into kindling to provide warmth for the Confederate soldier and Yankee soldier alike. When the soldiers died, graves were dug in the new Presbyterian cemetery for the unknown Yankee as well as for the unknown Rebel — and for the Indian — and for the Black —

General Kirby Smith sent a message TO THE SOLDIERS OF THE TRANS-MISSISSIPPI DEPT: "You have defeated a force three times your own...The path of glory is still open to you — call together your comrades, and shoulder to shoulder, we will yet free the soil of our beloved country from the invader's footsteps."

On the other side of the Mississippi River, General Sherman's army was marching toward the seacoast; on this side, Washington was on near-starvation rations.

51

There would still be another year of the war to live through, and there were all those mouths to feed on the plantations — all those people who had been strangers until they came to live under the same roof with one's own family. There were all those black slaves — they were still the children of their absent masters.

There were thirty families of women and children on the plantation of Thomas Carter Smith. Abner Smith, aged thirteen, kept to the fields — he had never heard so many shouting mothers and squalling babies in his life!

All the boys of thirteen were doing the work of men on the plantations. Many had become couriers in the army; they received the same pay as a soldier in the cavalry.

Medicines were needed so desperately. The women and girls had gone to the woods and stripped them of all sassafras root, mullein leaves, snake root — anything that could be boiled to make teas and poultices for the sick and wounded.

Now was the time to bring out those bales of cotton from under the protective sheds and take the cotton to Mexico for trade with the French Emperor Maximilian who had come to sit on a new puppet throne near the Port of Matamoras. William Etter was given the title of 'Colonel' and appointed State Military Agent in charge of a wagon train. Judge Daniel Ringo went along for the first journey in May.

Albert Pike, of the flowing locks and scribbling pen, came riding into Washington again, with oxcarts filled with his leatherbound books. He had been driven away from his mountain cabin by the advance of Colonel Thayer from Fort Smith. Judge Pike holed up in a room in the Etter home on Franklin Street and continued to translate from the Sanskrit, and write on his book concerning the rites and practices of the Masonic Order.

Albert Pike's son, Walter, had been brutally murdered the spring before, near the Missouri border, while on a foraging expedition with his company.

The town gave a ball for Albert Pike's daughters.

The colored population of the town gave a ball of their own. On the following day, Editor John Eakin received a letter. He published it in The Telegraph: "Dear Sir, I herewith, on behalf of the colored people of the town, enclose you eleven-hundred and forty-seven dollars, which they beg you to accept for the use of the sick and wounded in the hospitals. It is the proceeds from a ball given by them last night by permission of the proper town authorities.''

Colonel Etter and Judge Ringo came back over the Red River in September with four wagons filled with medicines and supplies. They had arrived in time for Judge Ringo to attend the General Assembly which Governor Flanagin had called to convene in Session Extraordinary.

Justices Albert Pike and Peyton English presided at the General Assembly.

As soon as the General Assembly adjourned the civil courts were held for Hempstead County. Judges Abner Bryson Williams and James R. Page presided.

Judge Thomas Hubbard had died during the summer. So had Judge George Conway. And Dr. Charles Mitchel — and Dr. James H. Walker.

Everyone was so tired.

When the military courts were held in the square white courthouse, the deserters and thieves and spies were convicted and hanged from the limbs of the catalpa trees in the courtyard.

Colonel Etter left with the second wagon train of cotton for trade at the Port of Matamoras, in Mexico, in November. The Federals were battling the Confederates near Brownsville, Texas — and on the other side of the Rio Grande the French were skirmishing with the Mexicans over Maximilian's puppet throne — but Washington needed food and medical supplies.

Three of the five Carrigan brothers had died in the war. Five of the Conway cousins were dead. Many many more were 'missing'.

Now and then someone would pause for a moment in the middle of Franklin Street and look over to the rise of the long hill beyond the Town Creek. Alchyny Delony had come walking down that hill after he had been missing for nine long months with nobody hearing a word from him. Maybe someone else would come walking --

At last it was April, 1865. The war was over for the other side of the Mississippi River. General Lee had surrendered to General Grant at Appomattox Courthouse on April 9. General Johnson had signed an armistice with General Sherman in North Carolina on April 7. On April 14, President Lincoln was assassinated. There was a new President of the United States — Andrew Johnson.

On May 2, General Kirby Smith called his generals together over in Marshall, Texas, and they, too, decided to lay down their arms. All except old Jo Shelby! When someone walked into his tent when he was still encamped at the Sandifur's farm near Fulton, and asked if he was going to surrender at Marshall, Texas, old Jo pistol-whipped the man right out of his tent. Then he had gone galloping over into Texas to start a colony of his own.

But that didn't last long. The war was over.

On April 28, the last casualty for Washington occurred near Brownsville, Texas. Colonel Etter, who had been waiting for a boatload of supplies to arrive from Havana so he could start homeward, was captured in the last week of the war and imprisoned, where he died of pneumonia.

Captain Ed Green, who had been fighting with the Confederate forces near the Rio Grande, had received permission to go inside the Federal lines and bury Colonel Etter. Then Ed Green came home with the supply wagons, and a red sash which a Mexican general had presented to Colonel Etter, and a little silver whistle that Colonel Etter had bought to bring as a gift for his twelve-year old daughter.

All four of William Etter's sons survived the Civil War.

RESCONSTRUCTION AND THE RAILROAD

1866 — 1890

WASHINGTON'S GREATEST YEARS AS the mother of illustrious sons and daughters came after the War Between The States, but so did her death blow. The winding tracks of the serpent "Railroad" began to come across Arkansas from the Mississippi River during the days of Reconstruction.

Reconstruction was not too difficult for Washington; she had been sent a good carpetbagger to govern her, named Robert MacWhorter, who had fallen in love with Miss Delia Conway, and married her, and become respected by all.

Washington also had her faithful Blacks. Archie Shepperson was elected Sheriff of Hempstead County; Richard Samuels was sent as representative from Hempstead County to the General Assembly (after Arkansas had been forgiven and allowed to rejoin the United States of America.)

The Whites knew their Blacks would watch after them. They could not be so certain of any turncoat or carpetbagger.

A Freedman's Bureau was set up in Washington with Edward Gantt in charge — the same Edward Gantt who had been a dedicated secessionist in 1861 when Arkansas seceded from the Union, but who had become an ardent Yank after General Steele captured Little Rock.

A school for Blacks was organized in the Baptist church. The Male Academy and the Female Academy had not reopened when the war was over but Alchyny Delony announced that he would open a school for white children in his home.

Everybody was too busy to pay much attention. They were all bankrupt. The fields were barren, the storehouses were empty. There was no livestock in the barns. The farm tools were worn out and the hands of the plantation owners held 'shinplasters', and Confederate money of other denominations, that were absolutely worthless.

There were still all those former slaves to think about. The white refugees had gone back to where they had come from but the Blacks had nowhere to go, and they had been told that they could now work for wages from their former masters. What wages?

Nonetheless, Washington survived, as every other town did in the South, and the lawyers of Washington began to make history again.

During the four years that Arkansas had been one of the Confederate States of America, four men of the town of Washington had represented her in the Confederate Congress at Richmond, Virginia — Dr. Charles Mitchel, Grandison Royston, Rufus Garland and Augustus Garland.

When the war was finished Augustus Garland set out to save all the lawyers of the south single-handedly. He went before the Supreme Court of the United States to test the validity of a law passed by Congress in January of 1865, which had effectively disbarred all lawyers who had borne arms against the North from practicing their profession in the United States courts.

This case, entitled EX PARTE GARLAND TEST OATH CASE, was decided by the Supreme Court in Garland's favor. The lawyers of the South could open the doors of their offices and earn their livelihood again.

In 1867 Ausustus Garland was elected United States Senator but was not allowed to take his seat in Washington, D.C.; Congress did not yet recognize representatives from all the southern states.

In the same year that Augustus Garland was knocking for admission at the door of the U.S. Senate, so was a childhood friend of his — George Williamson, who had moved to Shreveport some years before the war and had been elected U.S. Senator from Louisiana.

Both men went home to follow different directions.

Augustus Garland became governor of Arkansas.

George Williamson was appointed minister to Central America when Ulysses S. Grant became president of the United States.

Augustus Garland was destined to return to Washington, D.C. In 1877 he was elected U.S. Representative, and then United States Senator. This time he was allowed to take his seat. In 1885 he became the Attorney General of the United States in the cabinet of President Grover Cleveland.

When Augustus Garland moved over into the cabinet of President Cleveland, his seat in the U.S. Senate was taken by another young man from Washington — James Kimbrough Jones.

J.K. Jones had come to Washington after the Civil War to become a law partner with his friend (but no relation), Daniel Webster Jones.

Then, in the same way that the Garland brothers had risen into state and national politics, so did the two Jones men.

James K. Jones served as Speaker of the House of Representatives in the Arkansas General Assembly; he became United States Congressman and then United States Senator. For eight years he served as chairman for the Democratic National Convention.

Daniel W. Jones represented Hempstead County in the state assembly — was then elected Attorney General of Arkansas, and in 1890 became Governor of Arkansas for two consecutive terms.

Grandison Royston was called from retirement to serve as president of the Constitutional Convention of 1876.

Dr. Paul Booker was elected to the state legislature; so was Elmore Mitchel (Dr. Charles Mitchel's son), and Joel Conway (Judge George Conway's son), and James Ellis, James A. Williamson, Abner Bryce Williams, James Page and Burrell B. Battle.

Alfred Carrigan served another term in the General Assembly. Alfred Carrigan and James K. Jones were both appointed to the commission that chose the site and the plans for the huge white marble State Capitol with the golden dome and the golden doors that stands at the top of forty-eight steps on Capitol Hill in Little Rock.

Washington never knew when to stop.

The Blacks of Washington began to add to her history. Richard Samuels and Archie Shepperson both served in the state legislature. Archie Shepperson became a judge of the Hempstead County court; Bob Samuels, clerk of the county court; James Tyus, tax assessor.

The Blacks did not stop at politics. Richard Samuels founded the Colored Methodist Church Episcopal.

John Williamson, a former slave who had arrived with the Rev. Samuel Williamson, pastor of the Washington Presbyterian Church, had founded the Haygood Seminary for black students with the help of the Rev. Samuel Williamson and the Colored Methodist Church Episcopal. Five two-story frame buildings were built on a campus one mile down the road toward Fulton, and a curriculum set up for the education of black musicians, preachers and teachers. Prof. George L. Tyus, the first black man with a college degree to come into Arkansas, arrived from Payne College in Atlanta, Georgia, to become the first president of the seminary. Students came from the five surrounding states to attend this only boarding school of its kind in the land between the Arkansas River and Marshall, Texas.

Charley Shepperson would graduate from the Haygood Seminary and become the inspiration in the life of his stepson, William Grant Still, whose own symphonies, operas and ballet music would take him so far beyond Arkansas that he would be acclaimed as "the Dean of Negro composers of America."

Judge Abner Brice Williams, himself a Confederate State Senator and a member of the Utah Commission under President Cleveland, wrote of his home town:

> There is not a town between the seas of the same population that has ever turned out so many men distinguished for their ability in high and important positions which they have filled in the councils of state and nation.

In 1880 Washington achieved another "first" in her history — she reached her highest registered population figure on the census count — 780 souls.

In 1874 it was again decided that the courthouse on the crown of the hill was too small. A third Hempstead County courthouse was built — a two-story red brick building in the square on Franklin Street across the road from the Methodist Church.

They built a new jail in the block behind the Methodist Church.

A poorhouse was established on the road to Columbus.

But it was all too late. The railroad had finished winding its way across the prairies of Southwest Arkansas and a new town had been born eight miles south on the Prairie de Roane. The steel tracks had veered from the line of the Southwest Trail back near Arkadelphia and had by-passed Washington. It was said that many townspeople had argued that it was not necessary to offer the concession of a right-of-way to the railroad to make Washington the principal rail point for Hempstead County; others had insisted that the smoke from the engines would ruin the beautiful lace curtains and oriental rugs in the homes.

On February 19, 1875, a petition was filed before the county judge: "... with the county clerk, Thomas Simms, praying that the new town of HOPE might be incorporated. ."

Many old Washington names were on that petition — Carrigan, Jett, Cheatham, Ellis, Green —

In the same year, the first big fire swept through Washington. Some stores were rebuilt but they were smaller and of cheaper construction. A few of the storekeepers moved to Hope.

In 1883 there was a second great fire. A few more stores moved to Hope. Some of the townspeople began packing the beautiful lace curtains and oriental rugs and hauling them by oxcart to new homes in Hope.

The clock was running down for the little town on the hill of the five trails in the same way that it was running down for the last of the old-timers who had come down the Southwest Trail in the days of the Reverend William Stevenson and Stephen F. Austin.

Dr. Nathan Smith had died at the age of 77, two years after the Civil War. Daniel Witter, the first schoolmaster, died in 1886, at the venerable age of ninety-one.

The last to go was Judge Edward Cross; he died in 1887 on the plantation he called "Marlbrook" with a request that he be buried with a headstone carved in the shape of a stump, so he could be remembered as "one of the stumps of Arkansas."

James Black the silversmith, had died in 1872, a confused and sightless old man who was taken in by the family of Dan W. Jones after Dr. and Mrs. Isaac Jones died. It had been necessary to keep James Black confined in a small room off the kitchen in the Dan Jones home for the last two years of his life. Holes had been bored through the door and the wall, and chains passed through, so "Uncle Jimmy" could be secured and not allowed to wander off again and fall into the deep ravine in front of the Dan Jones home.

Through all the years that James Black had lived with Dr. Isaac Jones and his family, he had known that he could repay their kindness some day by giving them the secret of the processes by which he tempered the steel blades of his famous knives. James Black had waited until his seventieth birthday. Then he had called Dan Jones into his room and told him he wanted to give him his secret now. Dan Jones told the story himself in his later years:

> He stated that I was old enough and sufficiently well acquainted with the affairs of the world to properly utilize the secret, and that if I would procure pen, ink and paper, he would communicate his knowledge to me.
> I lost no time in bringing the materials to him. After sitting in silence for awhile he said, "In the first place" — and then stopped and began rubbing his brow with the fingers of his right hand.

59

He continued in this way for some minutes, as if trying to reconstruct something in his mind, and then, still rubbing his brow, said "Go away and come back in an hour."

I did so, but remained close to the open door where I could see him, and not for one moment did he take his fingers from his brow, or change his position.

At the expiration of the hour I went in and spoke to him. Without a perceptible movement, he said, "Go out again and come back in an hour's time." This I did, and the same process was again repeated, and again. When I came to him at the end of the third hour Mr. Black burst into tears, saying "My God! It is all gone from me! Daniel, there are ten or twelve processes through which I put my knives — but I cannot now remember even one of them...I have put it off too long."

James Black would live with Dan W. Jones for two more years, but from this moment on he was an insane old man — the struggle to communicate his secret had destroyed his mind.

The old tavern by the town well, reconstructed in 1961.

The Abraham Block house ca 1832.

The Washington Methodist Church, built in 1861.

The John D. Trimble house, built in 1852, restored in 1984.

The Washington Presbyterian Church, constructed in 1888.

The home built in Washington by Simon T. Sanders in 1845.

The Grandison D. Royston house, built in 1845.

The magnolia tree planted by Grandison Royston in 1839 at the site of his first home in Washington. The tree still blooms profusely each year.

The Augustus Crouch house before and after restoration in
1980. Augustus Crouch was a watch-maker in Washington
from 1840-1880.

The 1874 courthouse now houses the Information Center for the Old Washington Historic State Park.

A Black History Museum will be opened in the old office of Dr. Meeks. This house was moved into Washington from the town of Ozan, five miles to the north.

THE RESTORATION OF OLD WASHINGTON
1958

IN THE SPRING OF 1958 Washington was a place of a few old houses with memories — and vacant lots filled with weeds and underbrush.

There was only one block of stores left on Franklin Street. To the right was Jolly Stuart's Drugstore, Sandifur Dudney's General Store, a small frame postoffice with Mrs. James May as postmistress, Etter's Hardware Store where Mayor William Etter IV operated a printing press in the back room — an old brick bank building falling to ruins, and a little restaurant with tall arched windows that had been salvaged when the cupola of the 1874 courthouse had to be taken down after a tornado.

On the other side of the street, on the corner by the crossroads, was Doug Chism's Service Station. Next-door was a small frame grocery store with penny-candy cases owned by Fred and Letha Norwood, another little restaurant where Mrs. Lilla Porterfield was her own cook, waitress and cashier — a tin-sided store where M.E. Tate sold seeds from a tall oak cabinet with little glass doors — and a large two-story brick building that had once housed a merchandise store but which was empty now.

That was the business section of town.

On up Franklin Street, on the crown of the hill, stood the square white Hempstead County Courthouse built in 1836. It had become known as "The Confederate State Capitol" in 1929 after Mrs. Charlean Moss Williams and the Pat Cleburne Chapter of the United Daughters of the Confederacy persuaded the Arkansas Legislature to make an appropriation to restore it as a historic landmark.

Across from the Confederate State Capitol, on the other side of a vacant square, there was an enormous magnolia tree, and nearby was a derelict old house with a bandsawn wooden balustrade where Miss Mary Catts, the schoolteacher, had lived for fifty years.

There was no tavern at the crossroads any more. The long wooden two-story building where William Etter had once housed his family and The Washington Telegraph, had been condemned and torn down in 1943.

There was a well by the side of the road, with bricks falling away, and a wooden horse trough disintegrating in rot and decay.

Beyond the well was a little white Methodist church with a bell in the steeple that rang for services on the first and third Sundays of each month. In the middle of town, behind the ruins of the brick bank building, was the Presbyterian church where the bell rang for services on the second and fourth Sundays. The Baptist church in the curve of the road past the tavern was a new yellow tile church; the 1845 frame building with the four pillars hewed from four giant pines had blown away in a tornado in 1947.

The two churches founded by former slaves after the Civil War were still standing — the St. Paul's Christian Methodist Episcopal Church, an offshoot of the Colored Methodist Episcopal Church South — and the First Baptist Church of Washington, which stood on the rise of the hill where Elijah Stuart's tavern stood in 1829.

The red brick Hempstead County courthouse with the black iron numerals "1874" over the doorway had been converted into a schoolhouse in 1940 after the county seat for Hempstead County was moved to Hope. One mile down the road toward Fulton was the Lincoln High School, a legacy of the Haygood Seminary; Dr. Llewellyn W. Williamson, the grandson of the founder, was the Principal. The teachers in both schools were second or third-generation people of the hill; they bore the names of Stuart, Nash, Mitchel, Trimble, Etter.

There was nothing in particular to notice about the town of Washington as the cars came whizzing up Highway 4 from the direction of Hope: it was nothing more than a rise in the road where a yellow traffic signal flashed over the crossroads as a warning for the curve ahead around a yellow tile church.

On April 29, 1958, James H. Pilkinton, Chancellor of the Sixth Chancery Court, District of Arkansas, called a meeting of the townspeople in the Baptist church in Washington.

Judge Pilkinton practiced law in Hope, but he had spent his boyhood in Washington. Another lawyer from Hope came with Judge Pilkinton that evening — State Representative Talbot Feild, whose great-great-grandfather, Meredith Edwards, had been one of the five Town Commissioners who chose the hill of the five trails to be the seat of justice for Hempstead County in 1823.

Judge Pilkinton brought a film strip of the restoration of Williamsburg, Virginia, with him when he came to the meeting in Washington that April evening. He also brought color slides of the restoration of St. Augustine, Florida.

68

Judge Pilkinton and Talbot Feild told the townspeople that the State Highway Department had just announced that a transcontinental highway, which would span the continent from coast to coast, would pass through the fields between Washington and Hope within the next ten years. One sign on that new Interstate 30, the two men said, could direct travelers to turn down a ramp, drive eight miles north and "visit the cradle of Arkansas history — Washington, Arkansas."

But so much would have to be done first!

Judge Pilkinton and Talbot Feild then showed the slides of the restoration at St. Augustine, Florida, and the film strip of the restoration of Williamsburg, Virginia, to demonstrate what a dream could produce.

Two organizations were born in that April of 1958 — the Community Improvement Club, and a non-profit Foundation for the Restoration of Pioneer Washington, with Judge Pilkinton as president, Talbot Feild as secretary, and Mrs. Georgia Haynes as executive-secretary. The remainder of that first board of directors consisted of Alex Washburn, B. W. Edwards, William H. Etter, Mary Margaret Haynes, Thurston Hulsey, James May and Mrs. Mattie Trimble Wilson.

They were going to restore a town and they had not one dime in a treasury to do it with.

Mrs. Georgia Haynes had come to Washington to find a home in which to retire, and she offered to put herself and her antique furniture in Abraham Block's old home if the men of the town could lift the house to its feet again. It could be the first historic home to show to tourists.

But before the house could be restored the town must rise like the phoenix.

The Community Improvement Club set to work. Every man, woman, and child gave hours of volunteer manpower to the projects. Stores were repainted, vacant lots cleared of weeds and underbrush, flowers were planted, farms were "improved", schools and churches looked at with a critical eye, roads were blacktopped and new roads scraped and cleared. It was the beginning of time all over again.

Three short months later they were ready for the annual Fourth of July Homecoming in Washington. When aunts and uncles and cousins and friends gathered together they paid $1 for a chicken dinner prepared by the women of the town, and another $1 to tour the old houses where they had grown up as children. A brochure had been printed setting forth the plans for the future, and a blank check designed for those who wished to make a financial donation.

When the ledger was tallied up at the end of the 1958 Fourth of July Homecoming there was $1,000 in the treasury.

Work was commenced on the Abraham Block house. It was renamed the Block-Catts house in gratitude to Erwin Catts, of Atlanta, Georgia, who had donated the house and grounds in memory of Miss Mary Catts who had taught every one of those children who had returned for the Homecoming.

All winter long the men worked as they found time. By springtime the house had been lifted onto a new foundation, the bare lathes of the rooms had been replastered, the hand-planed floor boards scraped and waxed and polished, and Mrs. Georgia Haynes moved in with her Mallard bed and rosewood tables, her silver and fine china, her sconces and homespun coverlets.

The townspeople were ready to show their first historic home to tourists. Price of the tour — twenty-five cents.

The Block-Catts house was dedicated at the 1959 Fourth of July Homecoming. Twenty descendants of Abraham Block and Frances Isaacs Block came from Little Rock, Louisiana and points in Texas, to be the hostesses. There was a parade down Franklin Street, with surreys and carriages and even an oxcart. Mrs. Charlean Moss Williams made a speech from the courthouse steps and Mrs. Willie Mitchell, music director at the Lincoln High School, played the accompaniment for community singing on an old organ that had come across the Mississippi with one of the Fontaines many years ago.

Now other pieces of furniture began to come out of attics and storerooms from houses around the hill. A spinning wheel was found — it was placed in the front hall of the Block-Catts house. A mammy's cradle was located — it went in the upstairs bedroom of the Block-Catts house. One of the great-granddaughters of Dr. Nathan Smith donated his tall herb-cabinet — it would go in the tavern by the town well.

The tavern was to be the next project. The town well had already been bricked and curbed and a little shed placed over the top.

Mr. and Mrs. William R. King from Memphis, Tennesse, attended the 1959 Homecoming. Mr. King was president of the William R. Moore Dry Goods Company in Memphis; he was also president of the National Bank of Commerce and a director of the Illinois Central Railway. Mrs. King had grown up in Washington as Lucile Hart, great-granddaughter of Dr. and Mrs. Isaac Newton Jones.

During the 1959 Homecoming, Mr. and Mrs. King took James May aside and told him that the dedication of the townspeople had inspired them to join the project; when they left to return to Memphis they handed a check for $30,000 to James Pilkinton, to be used by the Foundation for the reconstruction of a tavern.

Ground was broken for the tavern in November of that year.

Anne Stingley Jackson, whose childhood had been spent in the Dan Jones home, had located measured drawings of the old tavern in the Library of Congress; they had been prepared as a part of the Historic American Building Survey in 1934. Two lots by the side of the tavern grounds were donated by the von Jagersfeld estate. (Carl von Jagersfeld, of Germany, had been a latecomer to Washington in the 1870's.)

More gifts of land were received. The von Jagersfeld estate also gave the site of the old Ebenezer Camp Ground. Margaret Black, of El Dorado, donated the towering magnolia tree which Grandison Royston had planted in the corner of the Isaac Newton Jones property when Dan Jones was six months old.

The Fine Arts Museum in Little Rock sent the portrait "A Southern Gentleman" painted by Jennie Delony Rice before she left Washington for New York and Paris where she became internationally known as a portrait painter and a miniaturist.

Books were found that had been written by Ruth McEnery Stuart; she had lived in Washington from 1875-1883 and used many of the scenes and people of the town in the "Simpkinsville" stories that became best-sellers in the turn of the century.

Mr. B. W. Edwards, of Hope, offered the loan of his rare gun collection if a place could be found to store it. Money was borrowed to restore the crumbling brick bank building and make it burglar-proof and fireproof. Later, Mr. Edwards donated half of his collection, the Foundation bought the other half, and the Edwards Gun Museum was established.

In 1958 the townspeople had invited Governor Orval E. Faubus to come see what was going to happen in the southwest corner of Arkansas; in 1959 they invited him back again to see what had already happened. When he came, they gave a $25 a plate Governor's Dinner and $5,000 was added to the treasury. It was used to pay the final bills for the restoration of the Block-Catts house.

From out in Albuquerque, New Mexico, Mr. Albert Simms, former United States Representative from New Mexico, and son of the Thomas Simms who had been "shot almost to pieces" at the battle of Wilson's Creek in 1861, sent money to build a birch fence around the old cemetery on the knoll behind Abraham Block's house. Albert Simms also sent another check to reconstruct the blacksmith shop where James Black had fashioned the wondrous Bowie Knife.

Everyone was contributing. The Confederate State Capitol was given another appropriation by the Arkansas Legislature and it became a museum for Civil War memorabilia. The women of the town had become guides for the tavern, the blacksmith shop, the Block-Catts house, the gun museum, the Confederate State Capitol.

The Monroes, Trimbles, Etters and Nelsons built a replica of a pioneer law office as a memorial to the lawyers of the town and filled the shelves with musty leather-bound volumes that had once belonged to Judge Thomas Hubbard, Judge Benjamin Jett, Judge Abner Brice Williams.

Mr. Olin C. Bailey, an oldtimer who had grown up "with the sand of Washington between my toes", left a bequest in his will for $18,000 to be used for the next project. Plans were made to restore the Simon T. Sanders home where Virginia Sanders had married Augustus H. Garland in 1852.

By 1965, both Mr. and Mrs. William R. King had died in Memphis, Tennessee. As a last gesture to the town of their childhood they left the greater portion of their estates for the "re-creation and perpetuation of the pioneer atmosphere in Washington, Arkansas."

In 1967, George Peck, president of the Commercial National Bank of Texarkana, became the second president of the Pioneer Washington Restoration Foundation. He gave six years of his time, and by 1973 it was found that the project had grown too large for volunteers to handle. The Arkansas State Parks and Tourism Department was brought in as a partner by the Arkansas Legislature. Washington became the "Old Washington Historic State Park." James Pilkinton resumed the presidency of the Foundation in 1974. Mrs. Georgia Haynes continued as the executive-secretary — she was eighty years old now, but she still conducted tours day after day through the Block-Catts house.

Mrs. Haynes died in 1981. Parker Westbrook, who had been a member of the Board of the Pioneer Washington Restoration Foundation since 1975, became the full-time volunteer executive-director.

Parker Westbrook, a descendant of an early Southwest Arkansas family, had recently retired after working for thirty years with congressmen in Washington, D.C., and for a governor of Arkansas. Recognized as one of the leading authorities in the state in the restoration and preservation of historic buildings, he was also the advisor from Arkansas to the National Trust for Historic Preservation, served as chairman of the Commission of the Arkansas Territorial Restoration in Little Rock, and was one of the founders of the Historic Preservation Alliance of Arkansas. He immediately began moving in historic buildings associated with Washington families and placing them where similar buildings had once stood, but which had long ago been lost to storms or fire.

The clock moves backward for Washington today. A Master Plan has been drawn up with the time-frame of 1824 to 1874. The Southwest Arkansas Regional Archives (SARA) has been established in the 1874 courthouse, where scholars and researchers come to study the unique history of the twelve Arkansas counties that once formed the original Hempstead County of 1819. A Black History Museum has been founded by the Ethnic Minority Memorabilia Association (EMMA) with Mildred Johnson Smith as the director.

Down on the new Interstate 30, there is a huge sign by the Hope Exit that reads "Old Washington Historic State Park." Thousands of visitors have driven down the ramp on the right, traveled eight miles north on Highway 4, paused for a moment at the crossroads where the big white tavern gleams in the afternoon sun — then turned up the Old Southwest Trail, past the few stores, and gone wandering on to the square white courthouse on the crown of the hill.

After a hundred and sixty years the travelers still come on.

Vehicles still travel up the old Southwest Trail past the square white courthouse of 1836, which was used as the Arkansas Confederate Capitol after Little Rock was captured by the Federal Army in September of 1863.

Southwest Arkansas Regional Archives. Highway 195 West, Washington, Arkansas.

REFERENCES USED IN PREPARING THIS BOOK

Frederick Gerstaeker, WILD SPORTS IN THE FAR WEST (London) 1854

George W. Featherstonhaugh, EXCURSION THROUGH THE SLAVE STATES (London) 1844

Louis Houck, HISTORY OF MISSOURI (Missouri) 1914

Josiah Shinn, PIONEERS AND MAKERS OF ARKANSAS (Little Rock) 1908

R.G. Thwaites, ed., EARLY WESTERN TRAVELS 1748-1846 (Cleveland) 1904

Fay Hempstead, HISTORICAL REVIEW OF ARKANSAS Vol. I

Walter Vernon, METHODISM IN ARKANSAS (Little Rock) 1976

Walter Vernon, WILLIAM STEVENSON: RIDING PREACHER (Dallas) 1964

Dallas Herndon, CENTENNIAL HISTORY OF ARKANSAS (Little Rock) 1922

John Gould Fletcher, ARKANSAS (Little Rock) 1947

Pat B. Clark, CLARKSVILLE AND OLD RED RIVER COUNTY (Texas) 1937

Grant Foreman, INDIANS AND PIONEERS (Oklahoma) 1975

Grant Foreman, INDIAN REMOVAL (Oklahoma) 1976

Marquis James, SAM HOUSTON (New York) 1929

Michael Dugan, CONFEDERATE ARKANSAS (Alabama) 1976

Fred Allsopp, ALBERT PIKE (Little Rock) 1928

Fred Allsopp, FOLKLORE OF ROMANTIC ARKANSAS Vol. II (Grolier Society 1931)

Thomas Staples, RESCONSTRUCTION IN ARKANSAS (New York) 1923

Jack Gregory and Rennard Stickland, SAM HOUSTON AND THE CHEROKEES (Arkansas) 1967

Farrar Newberry, A LIFE OF MR. GARLAND (Little Rock) 1908

Farrar Newberry, THE PLUMED KNIGHT OF ARKANSAS (Little Rock)

W.F. Pope, EARLY DAYS IN ARKANSAS 1895 (Little Rock)

John Henry Brown, THE ENCYCLOPEDIA OF THE NEW WEST

William Thorpe, BOWIE KNIFE (New Mexico) 1948

Noah Smithwick, EVOLUTION OF A STATE

Sam Williams, MEMORABILIA OF HEMPSTEAD COUNTY (from files of The Washington Telegraph 1886)

Margaret Smith Ross, Chronicles of Arkansas 46th Chronicle (Ark. Gaz. Nov. 1958)

DIARY AND LETTERS OF JOSIAH GREGG 1840-1847 (Norman Okla.) 1941

Dolphus Whitten, HISTORY OF HEMPSTEAD COUNTY Master's thesis 1940

The Washington Telegraph (Washington newspaper; Mexican File 1846; Civil War Years, 1861-1865; Borden File 1874

The Arkansas Gazette (Ark Post and Little Rock) 1819-1876

The Austin Papers - Vol. I, II (Annual Report of the American Historical Association) 1919

American State Papers (Washington) Vol. I, II, III

Territorial Papers of the U.S. Carter Vol. XIX, X, XV, 1819-1836

John L. Ferguson, A BRIEF HISTORY OF WASHINGTON (1972)

Robert and Pauline Jones, STEPHEN F. AUSTIN IN ARKANSAS, Ark. Historical Quarterly, Vol. XXV No. 4, 1966

J.H. Atkinson, FORTY DAYS OF DISASTER (Pulaski County Historical Society #1 Bulletin Series) 1955

Collections found at the Southwest Arkansas Regional Archives in Washington:
The Carrigan Collection, The Clark Papers, Nan Conway Brown Collection, Marguerite Smith Moses Collection, Etter Collection, Delony papers, Royston Collection, Fontaine Scrapbooks, Scrapbooks of the Washington Community Improvement Association (1959)

77

Santa Fe, 34
Scott, Sir Walter, 35
Sevier County, 30
Shaw, Anne, 9,28,29
Shaw, William, 3,6,9,28
Shelby, Jo, 47,51
Shepperson, Archie, 55,57
Shepperson, Charley, 58
Sherman, Gen., 51,53
Shields Family, 38
"Shinplasters", 45,55
Shook Family, 3
Shreve, Captain, 26,27
Shreveport, La., 27,31,47,50,56
Simms, Albert, 72
Simms, Albert Gallatin, 38
Simms, Mrs. Albert Gallatin, 36,38
Simms, Montcalm, 38,43
Simms, Thomas, 38,43,58,72
Simms, Zenobia, 36
Smith Family, 39
Smith, Kirby, 46,47,51
Smith, Mildred Williams, 73
Smith, Dr. Nathan, 6,39,48,51,59
Smithsonian Institute, 40,48
Southwest Trail,1-6,8,10,12,13,15,
    17,18,21,26,31,32,35,36,38,3-
    9,43,44,46,47,48,49,51,58,59,73
Southwest Arkansas Regional
    Archives, 73
Spain, 2,3,6,7,37
Spanish Trail, 7,34
Spring Hill, 27,31
Spring Hill Academy, 27
St. Paul's Christian Methodist
    Episcopal Church, 68
Steele, Gen. Frederick, 45,46
    49,50,51,55
Stevenson, Rev. William,3,4,5
    7,8,27,59
Still, William Grant, 58
Stuart, Abraham, 6
Stuart, Elijah, 6,7,33,68
Stuart Family, 39,69
Stuart, Jolly, 67
Stuart, Ruth McEnery, 71

Tate, M.E., 67
Tavern, The, 15,25,67,68,70,71,72
Taylor, Zachary, 24
Temperance Society, 31,37
Texas, 1,2,5,7,8,15,16,17,18
    19,20,21,22,2,24,29,30,32,70
Thayer, Gen., 51
Town Creek, 1,26,30,34,43,46,47
Trammell, Nicholas, 17,30,38
Trammell's Trace, 17
Trans-Mississippi Army, 46,47,51
Treaty of Guadalupe Hidalgo, 32
Trimble Family, 68,72
Trimble, John, 24

Trimble, William, 6,23
Tyus, Professor George L., 57
Tyus, James, 57

United Daughters of the
    Confederacy Pat Cleburne
    Chapter, 67
United States of America, 24,42,55
United States Congress,
    7,12,21,28,57
United States Marines, 32
United States Supreme Court, 56

Van Dorn, Gen., 44
Vaughn, 8
Vaughan, E.M., 13,45,48
Von Jagersfeld, Carl, 71

Walker Family, 39
Walker, Isabelle, 36
Walker, Dr. James, 23,24
Walker, Dr. Robert, 36
War of 1812, 1
War Between the States
    See Civil War
Washburn, Alex, 69
Washington Academy,
    Male & Female, 31,55
Washington on the Brazos, 8,16,22
Washington, George, 37
Washington Post Office, 12
Washington, Stephen, 37
Washington Telegraph,
    26,31,32,33,41,48,49,50,67
Westbrook, Parker, 72,73
Wilderness Road, 38
Williams, Abner Bryce, 57,58,72
Williams, Charlean Moss, 67,70
Williams, Sam, 41
Williamson, George, 56
Williamson, James A., 57
Williamson, John, 57
Williamson, Dr. Llewellyn W., 68
Williamson, Rev. Samuel, 37,57
Wilson Family, 3
Wilson, Col. John, 23,24,26
Wilson, Mrs. Mattie Trimble, 69
Wilson's Creek, Mo., 43,48,72
Witter, Daniel, 6,28,39,50,59
Woodruff, William, 49
Worsham, Billy, 43
Worsham Avengers, 44